under the

aikido

by Kisshomaru Ueshiba

Published by HOZANSHA Publications Co.,Ltd., Tokyo, Japan

Overseas distributors : Japan publications Trading Co.,Ltd.
P.O.Box 5030 Tokyo International, Tokyo 100-31, Japan

Distributors :
UNITED STATES : Kodansha America, Inc. through Farrar,
Straus & Giroux, 19 Union Square West, New York, NY 10003.
CANADA:Fitzhenry & Whiteside Ltd., 91 195 Allstate Parkway, Markham, Ontario L3R 4T8.
BRITISH ISLES AND EUROPEAN CONTINENT : Premier Book Marketing Ltd.,
1 Gower Street, London WC1E 6HA.
AUSTRALIA AND NEW ZEALAND : Bookwise International,
54 Crittenden Road, Findon, South Australia 5023.
THE FAR EAST AND JAPAN : Japan Publications Trading Co.,Ltd.,
1-2-1, Sarugaku-cho, Chiyoda-ku, Tokyo 101, Japan.

10

ISBN 0-87040-629-9

Printed in Singapore

As he stood by helplessly watching the tough hoods of the village beat up his father because of political differences, young Ueshiba vowed that he would never give up trying to become strong no matter what the cost in suffering and time. He would one day be able to handle them. One day they would flee in fear. He would have power.

And so his work began, eventually leading him to study everything he could about all the available arts of self-defense and martial science know as *budo.* Had this young, frail boy known the suffering and illness that awaited him, determined to slow down or defeat his ambition, he probably would have nevertheless continued his pursuit. The average man would have given up in a moment, but not Morihei Ueshiba. He fought against illness three or four times, each time painstakingly built-ing up his body after it had been worn down from the months of sickness.

Just to recover, however, was not enough for him. He sought outlets for his newly-regained youthful vigor. If others did twice as much work as ordinary people, he would do four times. During the traditional rice-making festivals in which specially cooked rice is pounded into flat cakes with a heavy, awkwardly-shaped wooden sledge, Ueshiba eagerly matched as many as ten strong young men. He would always win, usually ending the contest with such powerful blows that he would break the sledge. Ueshiba gradually grew dissatisfied with being only a strong man. He began to study jujutsu.

With jujutsu came an interest in learning and mastering the many different types of self-defense arts. Hard work, severe self-discipline and all the money he could possibly earn were poured into his mastery of these arts. He was granted certificates from several of the classical traditions.

Now he was strong. He had mastered the sword and the many arts of self-defense. Still, something was lacking.

Ueshiba's parents had raised him to have an extraordinary interest in the study of spiritual thought. From the time he was seven years old he had had some relationship with religious teachers. Yet even with this religious training young Ueshiba was unable to unite his spiritual beliefs with his physical accomplishments in swordwork and the empty-handed arts of self-defense.

After a lingering illness came the death of his father. Young Ueshiba was greatly sorrowed at the loss. He swore before the grave to break out of his mental deadlock, develop further, and uncover the secret of budo. From that moment his life changed greatly.

Sometimes the sad Ueshiba would stand on top of a mountain near his home dressed is white and reciting Shinto prayers. His old friends worried that he had gone mad. He himself realized that something, some unknown element, was still missing from his life. Finally he decided to enter a new Shinto sect lead by a preacher with whom he had been greatly impressed before his father's death. Taking his whole family he moved to a small house at the foot to the sect's central mountain near Kyoto and began a seven-year apprenticeship. He became the Holy Man's aid and confidant and even accompanied him on a danger-filled excursion to continental Asia that brought them to the brink of death. It was there, while staring death in the face, that he first became able to "see."

Returning to Japan, he resumed his former life of study and training at the small dojo that he had built in one part of his house. During the last year of his stay, a young naval officer and kendo teacher came to his dojo. The jujutsu man tried to explain the theory of his "Aiki" to the kendo man but it seems that the visitor had come for a fight. In the end, Ueshiba consented to having the match. The officer dashed forward to attack with his wooden training sword but each time Ueshiba was able to dodge the weapon with ease. Finally the challenger sat down without once toughing him.

After this Ueshiba went out into the garden and, standing under a persimmon tree wiping the perspiration from his face, he was suddenly overcome with a feeling which he had never experienced previously. He could neither walk nor sit. He was rooted to the ground in great astonishment. He recalled this experience:

> I felt that the universe suddenly quaked, and that a golden spirit sprang up from the ground, veiled me, and changed my body into one of gold.
>
> At the same time my mind and body became light. I was able to understand the whispering of the birds, and was clearly aware of the mind of God, the Creator of this universe. At that moment I was enlightened: the source of *budo* is God's love — the spirit of loving protection for all beings. Tears of joy streamed down my cheeks.
>
> Since that time I have grown to feel that the whole earth is my house and the sun, the moon and the stars are all my own things. I had become free from all desire, not only for position, fame and property, but also to be strong. I understood: *Budo* is not felling the opponent by our force; nor is it a tool to lead the world into destruction with arms. True *budo* is to accept the spirit of the universe, keep the peace of the world, correctly produce, protect and cultivate all beings in Nature. I understood: The training of *budo* is to take God's love, which correctly produces, protects and cultivates all things in Nature, and assimilate and utilize it in our own mind and body.

This experience revolutionized his life and gave birth to Aikido.

(From the detailed history included near the back of this book)

FOREWORD

In company with the popularization of Aikido, earnest wishes to know the true meaning of Aikido have arisen. "Aikido" and "Aikido Giho" were written to meet the demand of Japanese readers. This English edition is the revised translation of them.

I hope that you will understand that the essence of Aikido does not lie in fighting with others. The number of Aikido techniques explained here may count many. But the real number is much more and almost innumerable. Therefore it is left to the reader to acquire those other techniques through the explanations shown here. All study must be based on the correct understanding of Aikido principles, or mastery will be impossible.

Aikido trainees have been rapidly increasing in many parts of the world. It will be my pleasure, if this book serves to help those who study Aikido in places far from the Headquarters to enjoy their studies and solve their problems.

The members of Aikido Instruction Department, the translators and other dear friends who made possible this publication are heartily thanked.

Kisshomaru Ueshiba

Founder Morihei Ueshiba

Already a full twenty years have elapsed since the first edition of AIKIDO appeared in the English language. During those two decades we have seen far-reaching changes occur in the Aikido world. Most outstanding is the extraordinary growth in the popularity of the art outside of Japan.

Aikido now finds itself moving around the world alongside judo and karate-do as one of the modern international Japanese martial arts. Each year seems to bring new and bigger developments. I feel that this success is the result of a number of factors but the most important element must certainly be the philosophy of Aikido: a humanistic world view of the highest order which, along with the beauty and interest of Aikido movements, has captured the attention of intelligent people the world over. These people seem to realize that Aidiko lets them physically practice and train themselves in a philosophy of life that leads to 'spiritual prosperity.'

Aikido comes into being when the kind of strict training that results from confronting the instant of life and death is used as a stepping stone from which to leap above one's usual level. It is this self-discipline that relates so well to modern people who often find their spiritual life rootless and adrift as a result of contemporary stress and change. More-over, this severity of training, balanced and blended with the feeling of "Oneness with the Universe" that characterizes the Aikido approach, is seen as an expression of the best that is contained in Japanese *Budo*.

A look at our records tells us that in 1957, when the Japanese version of this book was first published, there were only about 2000 Aikido practitioners, worldwide, who had attained the rank of black belt. It was under those conditions that Mr. Kazuaki Tanahashi undertook the first translation into English. Now the number of belt holders has soared to over 40,000 in a total Aikido population of about one million. Such phenomenal expansion coupled with the new social conditions of today make it easy for the reader to appreciate just how necessary it was to under take a complete revision of this work. In doing so, we have added several important points to help make the book more complete, especially in relation to the essential nature of Aikido and its underlying spirit.

It is my sincere hope that this new version will uphold the honored place of the original as the first English book to introduce Aikido to the world. At the same time I pray that the new and expanded sections will provide a valuable and improved introduction not only to the physical techniques of Aikido but to its philosophical aspects as well.

Finally, I would like to take this opportunity to express my gratitude to all those whose painstaking efforts have gone together to make this republication possible. My thanks go to Mr. Larry E. Bieri, who completely revised and rewrote the text, and to the publisher who was so cooperative in every way.

October, 1984, Tokyo, Japan   Kisshomaru Ueshiba

Contents

INTRODUCTION

Aikido is The Way of Spiritual Harmony. The Founder, Morihei Ueshiba, originated it after having spent many assiduous years of research, practice and development. Aikido is the art of assimilation and unification with Nature. There is no duality, no struggle, no opponent. There is only a harmonious action of our own spirit with the spirit of the universe. The techniques of Aikido are the bodily realization of this harmony.

Aikido is the way of reconciliation. It is the bodily realization of the principle of the oneness of all beings. It is, as the Founder said, "the way of grand reconciliation and the compass which points toward, as is called in religions, Heaven or the Great Universe." This is also stated in one of his didactic odes:

> Graceful, graceful, all-important universe:
> One-Family Creation of the Lord of gods.

That is to say, do you need to start fighting in the state of no enemy, in the world of no opponent, in the creation of the Creator? It is the mission and the life of The Way to be one with the Center by having a sincere heart of love and reconciliation, and to construct a graceful "pureland" paradise in this world.

In order to attain The Way, we must experience the state of AIKI-VICTORY through unremitting practice. AIKI-VICTORY — or *masakatsu agatsu* — means, "Truth is victorious; therefore I am victorious." Having the conviction that Truth shall triumph we move forward with unshaken conviction to eliminate all the evil from this world, and further, to reach the state where there is neither right nor wrong. In doing this we also win over ourselves. When Truth has won and we have won over ourselves we have accomplished the mission which is given to every one of us. No self-contentment is allowed or possible if we are truly involved in this pursuit.

This mission is explained by the Founder in his didactic poems:

> Through Aiki, extend all your powers
> To achieve peaceful harmony with the world.

> Through Thy spirit Actions
> Lead, Absolve us Universal God.

> Destroy the foe that's hidden in the body.
> Lead all beings shouting out "hurrah!"

> By way of truth, perfect and know the Truth:
> Unity of all things seen-unseen

Throughout the history of Japan, Japanese have mutually agreed that the essence of *budo* (the martial ways) lies in its spirit. There are many examples where so-called master swordsmen ruined themselves because of their lack of self-control or the loss of their integrity. These records serve as a valuable warning for us that we should attain AIKI-VICTORY. Althrough the Founder made extensive studies of physical techniques, his spiritual study involved a series of bitter struggles and difficulties, and was many times more difficult. The more he studied the more he felt that force or technique only were inadequate. He could not find contentment with them. He had to enter the domain of the spirit and pierce a thick barrier in order to further develop himself and his thought.

The Founder says that he was inspired and felt himself as an incarnation of the golden Maitreya Bodhisattva. This was the start of Aikido. His words show that the secret of Aikido lies in the oneness of spirit, mind and body, which he acquired through bitter struggle. We see that the process of his study went from body to mind, and from arts to The Way.

We must remember, however, that Aikido is *budo*.

We must be strong. Whatever evil comes, we must be strong enough to sweep it away and protect justice. As Aikido is the realization of the Founder's achievement resulting from his endless study and practice; it agrees, in its essence, with the natural laws of the universe. It achieves the spirit of the universe. The entire body is full of this spirit. Great power, far beyond one's expectation, is there to be extended.

The Founder expounded, "This world is to be governed by man. It is the universe of man. If you shut your eyes, you see nothing. If you leave out your ego and your self-desire, the whole universe will be yours. Aiki is such an assimiliation of spiritual and bodily ways." It is the supreme state of Aikido to be one with the spirit of the universe. For this reason it is called the *budo* of unification and oneness.

The Founder also stated, "Aiki is the expression of Truth itself. It is the way of calling people together and reconciling them with love whenever they may attack us. When they angrily attack, smilingly reconcile them. This is the true way of Aiki." When you do not understnad this teaching, and use Aikido only for fighting, you will never obtain its secret. Perhaps you have grasped the general idea of Aikido by reading this introduction; however, its true meaning can only be realized through practice.

TECHNIQUES

— WAZA —

basic knowledge
— *KIHON* —

1. *KAMAE* (POSTURES)

All the natural, flexible movements of Aikido originate from correct postures.

These postures are *SHIZENTAI* (natural), *HIDARI GAMAE* (left), and *MIGI GAMAE* (right) stances; and the formal sitting position which will be explained later. These right and left *KAMAE* are also called *MIGI-HANMI, RIGHT OBLIQUE STANCE*, and *HIDARI-HANMI, LEFT OBLIQUE STANCE*. Natural stance is simply standing normally, with the entire body comfortably balanced. It is simply that from which you move into a left or right stance.

Left stance is an oblique posture, with the left foot placed a half step ahead of the right. The entire body should be flexible, without tension, and ready to counter any changes. In Aikido when you assume this position, your body needs to be in a "*SANKAKU-TAI*" (triangular-form). Remember, an equilateral tetrahedron is the most stable form, and one which changes into a sphere when turned or spun.

Right stance is the exact opposite of left stance.

SANKAKU-TAI, HIDARI-HANMI

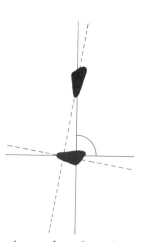

An equalateral-tetrahedron

MA-AI

2. *MA-AI* (DISTANCE)

When you face your opponent and engage him at a DISTANCE it will be clear that ideal distance means to utilize sufficient space in which to maneuver easily. The movement of mind, the FLOW OF KI, as well as the actual space between and direction of movement of the two persons are all delicately related to *MA-AI*.

In Aikido training, DISTANCE is considered proper if the hands of the two are just able to touch each other. However, proper *MA-AI* varies according to relative stances. There are basically two possible combinations of stances. These are

AI-HANMI or MUTUAL OBLIQUE STANCE in which both persons are standing in either RIGHT OBLIQUE STANCE or LEFT OBLIQUE STANCE; and *GYAKU-HANMI* in which one person is standing RIGHT and the other is LEFT.

When setting up proper *MA-AI*, assume and maintain a face to face relationship regardless of your movements. Take advantage of the surroundings, such as the light from the sun or a window, a line on the floor or other features, and bring the opponent into your *MA-AI*.

AI-HANMI
(HIDARI)

GYAKU-HANMI
(HIDARI)

TEGATANA

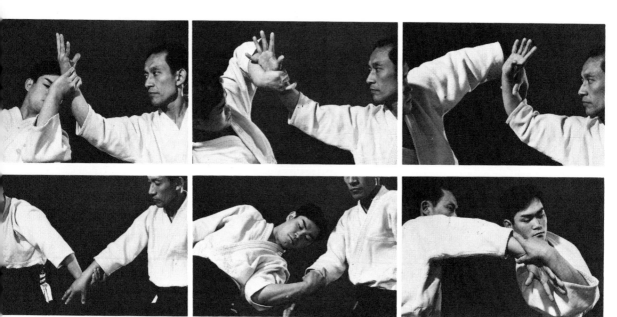

Examples of using the handblade from *ONE HAND GRASPED*

3. *TE-SABAKI, TE-GATANA* (HANDWORK and the HANDBLADE)

There is little difference between the movements of Aikido and those of Japanese swordsmanship. In Aikido, the hand itself is used as a sword. In many movements of Aikido the hand is used as a *TEGATANA,* or HANDBLADE. There is no other *BUDO* that employs the *TEGATANA* so often as Aikido. In a broad sense, "HANDBLADE" includes the part of the arm reaching from the tip of the little finger to the elbow, but it is usually used to indicate the part reaching from the tip of the little finger to the junction of the hand and wrist. This part of the arm is directed by *KOKYU-RYOKU,* BREATH POWER, which "flows" from the center of the body, the CENTRUM. When accompanied by proper BODY MOVEMENT (*TAI-SABAKI)* there is a powerful EXTENSION of BREATH POWER. This EXTENSION is greatly emphasized in Aikido.

All the basic techniques of Aikido such as *UDE-OSAE* (ARM PIN) and *KOTE-MAWASHI* (WRIST OUT-TURN) employ HANDBLADE action. Its use is one of the secrets of the arts of attack and defense; examples of which include deflecting a thrust, suppressing the opponents's elbow, and cutting upwards or hooking downwards on his wrist. It is applied to striking, twisting, pulling and pushing with the hands. All of these together we call *TE-SABAKI,* or HANDWORK.

4. *KI NO NAGARE* (The Flow of the FLOW OF KI)

"*KI*" is one of the core concepts of Oriental thought which has contributed to the high standard of philosophy that we in Asia have inherited from the ancient past.

Moreover, it was believed by our ancestors that "*KI*" was life itself. It is a way of conceptualizing the LIFE FORCE or the power of the SPIRIT. Even today in our daily lives we use many words which reflect this inheritance. For example, we feel that nothing can be accomplished if a person has "dropped his *KI*" (to be dispirited), or if his "*KI* withers" (to be in low spirits). Illnesses in Japanese characters may be literally read as "diseased *KI*" and thus is linked in our minds with death.

When it is possible to freely activate and exhibit to the maximum the *KI* that any human being possesses, it leads to an unexpectedly strong power. It also allows him to live the freest and most vigorous life of which he is capable. Here in lies the significance of the existence of Aikido, for correct training in the art teaches a person to become able to manifest his *KI* freely.

In order to master this feeling, the *KI* that is the content of human "BREATH POWER," and the original *KI* that is omnipresent in the universe should be in accord. The distinguishing characteristic of Aikido movements is that they harmonize with the order of the universe and adjust spontaneously to its changes. Therefore in Aikido one trains with the aim of realizing the unification of the individual *KI* with that of the universe by fostering *KOKYU-RYOKU,* BREATH POWER. When this BREATH POWER is extended from all the parts of the body and sent out through both the HANDBLADES, the techniques of Aikido become alive and display their full worth. This in turn leads a person to become an embodiment of the totality of nature.

It is impossible to make the form of Mother Nature concrete in oneself if your movements are trapped inside the ego. One should lead the opponent and become one with him while in the state of mind that is often called "the Realm of No-Self," for it is here that one feels the living *KI* flow. When someone is able to master Aiki technique such that he has it freely at his command, he will move the opponent any way that he may will by means of the living FLOW OF KI. He has learned to take the FLOW of the opponent's *KI* into his own and control him through this unity rather than by opposition.

This correct use of the FLOW OF KI can only be mastered through constant training in Aikido, and unrelenting effort at fostering BREATH POWER. Thus we may define the FLOW OF KI to be the state in which the total LIFE FORCE that is allotted to any human being is being displayed to the fullest extent possible.

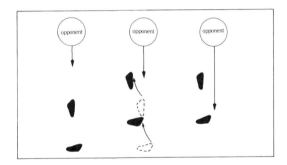

5. *IRIMI* (ENTERING)

The art of ENTERING is utilized during the instant of your opponent's attack. It means to move out of his line of attack to his SHIKAKU or "BLIND SPOT." For example, if the opponent comes to thrust or stab you with his right hand, put your left foot a step forward to his right while standing in a LEFT OBLIQUE STANCE. Thus you have side-stepped his attack, and can hit his side with your left fist and his face with your right. In this way you strike him with great force, the combination of his attacking momentum and your forward movement. The ENTERING principle is basic to most movements of Aikido, for the postures and the movements of Aikido mainly consist of *OBLIQUE STANCES* which are adapted from the art of using the spear.

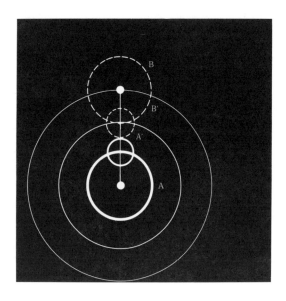

A : your body
A' : your hand
B : opponent's body
B' : opponent's hand

6. *TAI-SABAKI* (BODY MOVEMENT)

In Aikido, if your BODY MOVEMENT is correct, you become similar to a spinning top. At all times you try to get your opponent involved in turning around your center axis. This movement must be positive, spherical and smooth, no matter what force attempts to interfere with it.

Your body is thought of as an exquisite machine.

If your toe moves rightward, every part of your body follows the movement of the toe and changes its form in a unified fashion.

Through *TAI-SABAKI*. you get your opponent into your spherical movement and guide him at will, like a spinning top throws off things which touch it.

7. *CHIKARA NO DASHI-KATA* (THE EXTENTION OF POWER)

The reason that Aikido may be practiced and skillfully applied even by older, weaker or smaller persons is that the movements of Aikido are natural, rational actions. Actions that manifest a unity of KI, mind and body are the ideal of the art. It is training toward this state that is important in Aikido practice. As an example, suppose that you stretch out your arm and using all the energy and power you have, try to prevent someone from bending it. You will find that your friend will have little trouble making it fold at the elbow despite you resistance.

Next, open your hand and imagine that your power is directed from your *SEIKA TANDEN,* your *CENTRUM,* the "one point" which is the body's center of gravity and the point of concentrating your power. This point is the area in the center of your lower abdomen, just below the navel. Extend your arm with the feeling that your power is flowing from this point up through your arm and out the tips of your fingers. Don't let it stop or bunch up at your shoulders or elbow. Instead, relax them imagining that they are only passageways for your strength. This time your friend will find it surprisingly difficult to bend your elbow. When you thoroughly and willfully concentrate your power and extend it out toward the other person, the effect is unexpectedly strong.

As shown in this example, the extension of your power depends on the state of your CENTRUM. The power from a stable CENTRUM is inspired by fullness of spirit, and passes through every part of the body flowing outward. Therefore in Aikido we say *"CHIKARA O DASU,"* "EXTEND POWER," rather than *"CHIKARA O IRERU,"* "USE FORCE." Your power should not be inactive because, like standing water, it becomes stagnant. Instead, it must be like a stream, flowing energy from your body through the tips of your fingers, your toes, even from the glitter of your eyes, sending it out toward the subject. This is a power that is not simply USING FORCE. EXTENDED POWER is the overall power of oneness that a person can manifest and use once he has unified his *KI,* mind and body.

If a trainee of Aikido thinks it is proper to USE FORCE and grips and pulls his training partner, he is wholly mistaken. If you try to pull your partner toward your side, he will reflexively pull back and you have nothing more than a tug-of-war, FORCE against FORCE. Even a person who can lift 200 kilograms but does not know how to utilize power will be bewildered with the overall, unified and EXTENDED POWER of an Aikido-trained child who may be capable of lifting only 20 kilograms. From the very first, you should use your Aikido study to learn how to EXTEND POWER smoothly from the CENTRUM out through every part of your body, your fingers and toes. In this way your whole body will be stable but not stiff or rigid.

8. *UKEMI* (BREAKFALLS)

The BREAKFALL is an art of self-defense to soften the shock of falling when the balance of your body is lost. It is the way of using the movement of the opponent's force, following its direction actively and avoiding the resistance of the ground or other injury. There are:

MAE-UKEMI,	FRONT BREAKFALLS;
USHIRO-UKEMI,	BACK BREAKFALLS;
YOKO-UKEMI,	SIDE BREAKFALLS.

FRONT BREAKFALLS: Walk forward naturally and turn the fingers of your leading hand to the inside. In BREAKFALLS, the leading hand should on the same side as the forward-most foot. Thrust this leading hand in a forward, down and backward arc much as if bending down to reach

MAE-UKEMI

USHIRO-UKEMI (BACK BREAKFALL)

around a large barrel, and then follow its path with your body turning like a wheel. Roll on the outside of your arm, elbow and shoulder, and on along a diagonal line across your back to your hips and legs.

BACK BREAKFALL: Draw in your chin tightly, bend your knees and roll backward smoothly with rounded hips, waist and back, landing in a ready-to-stand position. Variation: Roll on the ground as before but only as far as the base of your neck. Then rebound and roll back forward to your original starting position, standing in either *KAMAE*.

SIDE BREAKFALL: Slide your right foot obliquely in front of your left foot, lower your left knee and fall rightward, striking the mat with your out-stretched right hand, palm down, to accommodate the resistance of the ground and reduce the shock to a minimum.

FRONT and BACK BREAKFALLS are most commonly used because they are more natural and because the techniques of Aikido are based on principles of SPHERICAL ROTATION. Falling is most important and there is a Japanese expression which states, "BREAKFALLS for three years." However, special practice periods for BREAK-FALLS are not necessary because in Aikido they are practiced during the exercise of other techniques. Thus you learn them naturally.

9. *ZA-HO* (SITTING METHOD)

"Sit squarely when indoors" used to be a principle for Japanese warriors of the feudal period. Their manner of sitting squarely (*SEIZA*) and walking on the knees ready against enemies (*SHIKKO*), were the basis of *budo*—the principal accomplishment of warriors. This can be understood more easily if you remember that in their homes Japanese usually sit on *tatami* straw-mats, even in present-day Japan. Naturally the study of *SEIZA*, SITTING, is important when training in Aikido as it is based on the *budo* which arose spontaneously during the daily lives of Japanese warriors. It is also good training for legs and loins, and for developing a skillful carriage of the body—an important point in Aikido. Much like with the "groundwork" in judo, if SITTING TECHNIQUES (*SUWARI-WAZA*) in Aikido can be managed at will, executions from a standing position will be much easier. When sitting, put your left big toe on your right big toe and sit on your archs in a straight form. The space between your knees should be the width of two fists. Movements which begin from this form must be harmonious and united. The movement of the CENTRUM leads that of your whole body as explained in the section on "BODY MOVEMENT." One of your knee joints will function as the axis of your *TAI-SABAKI*.

DOSHU KISSHOMARU UESHIBA

basic preparatory exercises

TANDOKU DOSA (SOLO EXERCISES)

Individual exercises in Aikido are practiced without an opponent. Because they are done by oneself one must be careful or they are apt to be mere empty movements lacking the spiritual fullness which is most important in Aikido.

1. ASHI-SABAKI (FOOTWORK)

A calm and stable mind is absolutely essential to Aikido, but just as important is a stable body. Hence special attention must be given to ASHI-SABAKI or FOOTWORK.
A stable CENTRUM must always follow the movements of the feet. The feet should be carried lightly along the ground, as though one were walking on water. It is important to move on the balls of the feet as much as possible.

TSUGI-ASHI (SHUFFLE STEP)

Put your right foot forward and before stepping down on it firmly, quickly slide your left foot up behind it, planting both feet at almost the same time. Keep the body stable. In the case of MIGI-HANMI (RIGHT OBLIQUE STANCE), your left foot always follows the right. Likewise, for movements in any direction; right, left, forward or back; the trailing foot remains behind the leading foot at the distance of a natural stance. This SHUFFLE STEP often accompanies such techniques as SHIHO-NAGE (FOUR SIDE THROW), IRIMI-NAGE (ENTERING THROW) and so on.

AYUMI-ASHI (WALKING)

This type of WALKING is the same as ordinary walking with one exception: the foot which is moved forward is pointed to the outside.
WALKING, fundamental to all basic Aikido techniques, is mostly used in the movements of UDE-OSAE (ARM PIN) and IRIMI-NAGE (ENTERING THROW).

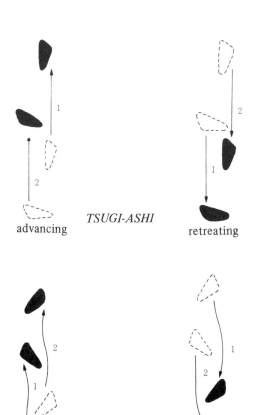

advancing   TSUGI-ASHI   retreating

AYUMI-ASHI

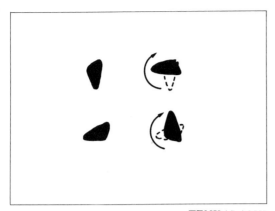

TENKAI-ASHI

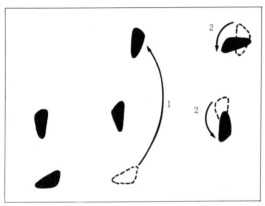

KAITEN-ASHI

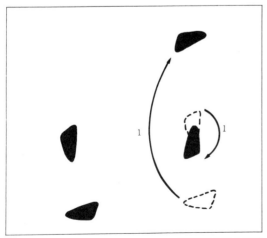

TENKAN-ASHI

TENKAI-ASHI (PIVOT)

PIVOT means to turn from one OBLIQUE STANCE to the other OBLIQUE STANCE simply by rotating your vertical axis, without stepping or moving out of the area where you are standing. For example, from LEFT OBLIQUE STANCE, you turn your face and body 180° rightward and assume a RIGHT OBLIQUE STANCE. You are now facing in exactly the opposite direction. If you master this movement without your hips "floating" or "bouncing" you will be able to change your stance and respond to any opponent without unbalancing your CENTRUM. The key to TENKAI-ASHI is to balance at both knees and turn on the balls of the feet. The feet do not step in this BODY CHANGE.

These next two movements are similar to the PIVOT but use a step forward or backward in combination with it. They can be executed from LEFT or RIGHT OBLIQUE STANCE.

KAITEN-ASHI (FORWARD-STEP PIVOT)

When in a LEFT OBLIQUE STANCE put your right foot a step forward, then turn your hips and body leftward 180° and again assume a LEFT OBLIQUE STANCE. Techniques based on this movement are *IRIMI-NAGE* (ENTERING THROW), *KOTE-MAWASHI* (WRIST IN-TURN) and others.

TENKAN-ASHI (PIVOT BACKSTEP)

When in a LEFT OBLIQUE STANCE, turn 180° to the right around your leading left foot by swinging your right foot around as if stepping backwards. You should end in the same LEFT OBLIQUE STANCE but facing in the opposite direction.

Note:

- In this book the verb "to pivot" may be used to indicate any of these three movements. However, if upper case letters are used, i.e. PIVOT and so on, the terms should be taken as a technical "jargon" with the precise meaning explained on this page.

Refer to pages 30, and 34 to 38 for more details about TURNING.

Keeping both feet under the hips

SHIKKO (KNEE WALKING)

KNEE WALKING means to move your body while in the SITTING STANCE called *KIZA*. As sitting is a keynote of Aikido, KNEE WALKING is an important basic movement. The rule in Aikido is OBLIQUE STANCES. Proper SHIKKO is to move forward or backward on a line, assuming alternating LEFT and RIGHT OBLIQUE STANCES. To start from a LEFT OBLIQUE STANCE, for example, move from SEIZA to *KIZA* by standing up your feet under your buttocks so that your weight is resting on the balls and toes of the feet and your knees. Imagine a straight line running from between your feet across the room. Now put your left knee forward and down onto the imaginary center line, pivoting on the right knee. Keep a straight upper body and move your right foot along with the left foot keeping both of them under your hips as you assume the LEFT

OBLIQUE STANCE. Continue the movement with your right knee moving forward to the center line and so on. Try to keep the feet together and under your hips as much as possible. In KNEE WALKING, a 180° turn is made by first changing to a one-knee/one-foot stance. For example, if in a LEFT OBLIQUE STANCE, shift the right leg from a knee-down to a foot-down stance by twisting your body to the right. Now you are balanced on the left knee and toes, and the right foot. Next turn your body further rightward by moving the right foot and pivoting on the left knee until you have turned 180° around. Return your right knee to the mat and assume a RIGHT OBLIQUE STANCE. Always begin and move with stability. Even a slight unbalancing must never be a part of *SHIKKO*.

2. *TAI NO HENKA* (BODY CHANGES)

BODY CHANGING is a process which is basic to the acquiring of Aikido techniques. There are four ways to change from both left and right stances. From these movements there are an almost unlimited number of possible variations.

LEFT CHANGE 1
Assume a LEFT OBLIQUE STANCE hold out your left hand naturally, on a level with your CENTRUM, palm down. Turn your body 1/2 circle rightward, pivoting on your left foot and drawing right foot backward in a circular movement. As you move reverse the position of the hand so that when the turn is completed the palm of your left hand will be up. During the entire movement always allow your POWER to flow from the CENTRUM through every part of the body and out

through the tips of your fingers.

LEFT CHANGE 2
From a left stance, move to a right stance by putting your right foot forward. Raise and hold out both hands as explained above. Keep them at a height a little lower than the chest.

LEFT CHANGE 3
From a left stance, put your right foot a step rightward and assume a right stance facing to the right. The hand motion is same as above.

LEFT CHANGE 4
From a left posture, turn to the left using the foot work shown below, and assume a right oblique stance. In this case, pivot on the left foot, executing the 270° circular movement with harmonious unity of the upper and lower body. Practice the corresponding Right Changes, too.

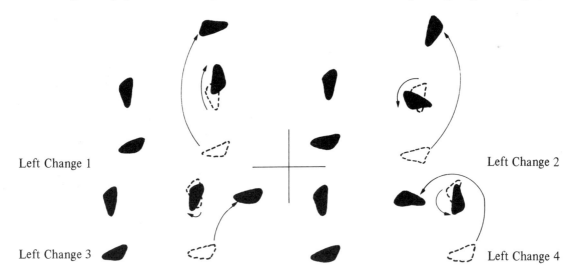

Left Change 1

Left Change 2

Left Change 3

Left Change 4

Change 1 (basic *TENKAN*, see p28)

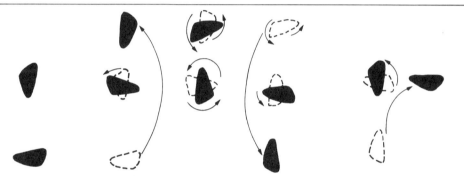

3. *KOKYU NO HENKA* (BREATH CHANGES)

BREATH CHANGING is an exercise that trains you in EXTENDING POWER in concert with the changes of our body and without any delay. In Aikido the exertion of the united powers of mind and body is called *KOKYU* (BREATH) from the viewpoint that it must be in accord with the constant breathing or rhythm of the whole body. Thus the power which is exerted from the whole body is called *KOKYU-RYOKU* (BREATH POWER).

LEFT BREATH CHANGING

Assume a left posture. Put your right foot a step forward taking a RIGHT OBLIQUE STANCE while concentrating your whole power at your CENTRUM. Hold your hands as HANDBLADES and swing them up and outward to a position level with your eyes as you move. EXTEND POWER

from the CENTRUM, through the chest, shoulders, elbows, and out of the tips of your fingers. The axis of this movement series is your left foot and the balance point is at the hips (*KOSHI*). Now turn your body 180° to the left, PIVOTING on your left foot. While turning, move your hands down in an arc and then swing them up again as you step out on your right foot. Turn 90° rightward, and repeat the above movements. This Aikido exercise is for EXTENDING POWER through the unity of mind and body, and harmony between the movements of hands and feet, all balanced at the hips.

Unless a continual flowing movement is executed from the beginning to the end, it will not be an exercise of BREATH POWER (see above photos). RIGHT BREATH CHANGING is simply the reverse of left.

4. *KOKYU TENKAN-HO* (BREATH TURNING)

To swing the HANDBLADE up and down in a cutting motion while executing the same FOOT-WORK (*ASHI-SABAKI*) as in BREATH MOVE-MENT is called BREATH TURNING. This is a bodily rendition of the changes found in the techniques of Aikido swordwork and is the basic preparatory exercise for *SHIHO-NAGE* (FOUR SIDE THROW), one of the typical throws. As it is a drill in continuously changing the body, used for cutting on all four sides, special care must be taken not to break the FLOW OF KI.

LEFT BREATH TURNING
From a LEFT OBLIQUE STANCE swing your HANDBLADE up and then cut down as you step forward on your right foot. Swing your HAND-

BLADES up again, PIVOT 180° (*TENKAI-ASHI*) leftward and cut down again as your right foot steps forward and you assume a RIGHT OBLIQUE STANCE. Now raise your HANDBLADES, PIVOT 90° to the left and again step out on your right foot and cut down; raise your hands, PIVOT 180° left, step and cut to complete the series of cutting in the four major directions. In this drill the movement of the hands is very important. They must be moved so that BREATH POWER is spiraled out from the tips of your hands, as explained in the section on BREATH MOVEMENT. When swinging up, lead with your thumb and breathe in; and when swinging down, lead with your little finger and breathe out. RIGHT BREATH TURNING is just the reverse of the left.

Wrist in-turn (*NIKYO*) exercise (1)

5. *TEKUBI KANSETSU JUNAN-HO* (WRIST JOINT FLEXABILITY EXERCISES)

The human body must move harmoniously, from head to foot. For example, if the forefinger turns rightward, the whole body must be able to follow this movement. Therefore our wrist joints must be flexable enough to follow the movements of our hips and feet. Some example exercises follow.

KOTE-MAWASHI-HO (*NIKYO*)
(WRIST IN-TURN EXERCISE)
Grasp your right hand lightly with your left hand and hold them up as high as your chest, about a foot away from your body. Turn your right wrist outward, with your left thumb covering the base of your right thumb. Push up the right hand, and twist it outward. Pull in both your elbows at the same time. Then when you loosen your grasp and stop the upward force, your right hand will go back to its original position by reflex. In this case you should relax your shoulders. Your right hand must be in a state of torsion when you twist it with your left hand.
This exercise loosens the hand muscles which are

Wrist in-turn exercise (2)   Wrist out-turn (*KOTE-GAESHI*) exercise

not used daily, exercises the arm muscles and your chest, and quickens the circulation of the blood. It is the basic exercise for the Aikido technique of *KOTE-MAWASHI* (WRIST IN-TURN). Exercising of the left hand is the same.

KOTE-GAESHI-HO
(WRIST OUT-TURN EXERCISE)

Hold up your right hand as high as your chest, about a foot in front. Turn it palm up. Put your left thumb on the back of your right hand a little below the roots of the ring and little fingers. Grasp the root of your right thumb by the other fingers of your left hand. Then EXTEND POWER through your left hand and fingers and twist the right hand while moving your left elbow gently down toward your body.

In this case also, you should be careful to relax your body and EXTEND POWER exactly at the tips of your left fingers when you twist the right hand. This movement is accomplished by using the leverage of your left thumb and other fingers

(mainly the little finger). When you release your power, your right wrist returns to its original position by reflex.

Repeat these exercises many times.

This is the basic exercise for the technique of *KOTE-GAESHI* (WRIST OUT-TURN). Exercising of the left hand is the same.

TEKUBI SHINDO
(WRIST SHAKING CAPILLARY EXERCISE)

Hold out your hands in a horizontal position and shake them vigorously.

When you feel tired, relax your arms and put them down. Then shake the entire arm in the same way. Repeat these movements many times.

These three exercises have the effect of making your joints flexible and strong and are similar to various other medically accepted exercise methods. It is advisable from the medical viewpoint to do such preparatory exercises before going into the technical practice of Aikido.

SOTAI DOSA (PAIRED EXECISES)

There are various basic preparatory exercises for
the movements of Aikido which are practiced
together by two persons. Because we end each
movement in this exercise before going into the
next action, we are apt to feel that each is merely
a separate movement. But the essence of this
exercise is to flexibly move your body with the
feeling that your movement continues without
severing the unseen tie between you and your
opponent. In this way a flexible action, which
directs the opponent's motion at will, can be
acquired. It is just such actions that are the basis
of all Aikido techniques.

TAI NO TENKAN-HO (OUTWARD TURNING)

1. TAI NO TENKAN-HO (BODY TURNING)

ENTERING and TURNING are the main movements of Aikido. If BODY TURNING can not done at will, it is bound to become a great obstacle in technical training.

BODY TURNING means to turn the body on either foot in order to change the position of the whole body in a circular movement.

KATATE-TORI TENKAN-HO (ONE-HAND-GRASPED BODY TURNING)

This technique is used to move on your left or right foot to the safest and easiest position from which to control an opponent who has grasped at your left or right wrist. First you and your partner assume an OPPOSING OBLIQUE STANCE (GYAKU HANMI) your left wrist grasped from the outside by the opponents right hand.

You should particularly notice that this movement has begun before your hands touch each other and it is constantly guided by the unseen tie of spirit/mind. That is to say, a movement without this feeling of the unseen tie is meaningless. Some of the variations developed from this posture are as follow.

OUTWARD TURNING

Turn your body on your left foot about 180° rightward with full BREATH POWER and extend your hands, allowing BREATH POWER to flow naturally from the CENTRUM out through the fingers. The opponent will then follow to your left rear (see lower photos).

INWARD TURNING

Turn your body on your left foot about 90° rightward and EXTEND POWER flowingly through your fingers.

SIDE TURNING

Turn your body on your left foot about of a 270° rightward in the same manner as OUTWARD TURNING.

BACK TURNING

Turn your body on your left foot one complete circle rightward in the same manner as in OUTWARD TURNING.

BODY TURNING EXERCISES must be executed with a stable form centered at the hips, with a full spirit and flexible body, just as in other exercises of Aikido. Changing on the right foot is the reverse of the above.

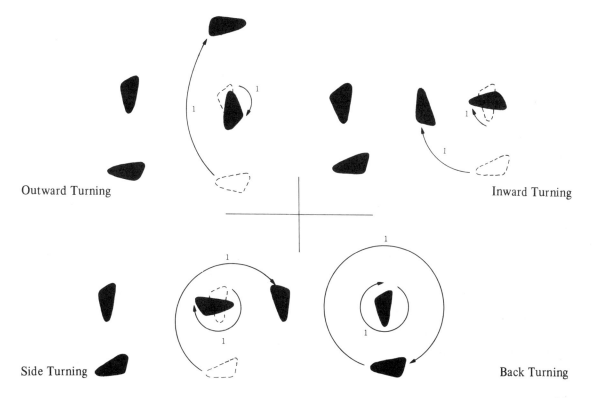

Outward Turning   Inward Turning

Side Turning   Back Turning

RYOTE-TORI TENKAN-HO (BOTH HANDS GRASPED BODY TURNING EXERCISE)

Your hands are grasped by an opponent standing in front of you. You respond by moving your weight to one or the other of your feet to move off the center line and swing your hands up over your head. You then step in, PIVOT around your vertical axis 180° and cut down with both hands. The key points in performing these drills are:

    1. The spiritual tie between you and the opponent.

    2. EXTENDING POWER.

    3. A realization of the oneness of Aikido, which is the united movement of body and mind.

    4. A basic expression of the oneness of sword and body, originating from the idea that the sword is but the extention of the body—which can be applied to the techniques of Japanese swordsmanship.

FRONT TURNING

Assume a MUTUAL LEFT-OBLIQUE STANCE. When both your hands are grasped by the opponent, put out your left foot somewhat forward and to the left while swinging up both HAND-BLADES in a spiriling motion and EXTENDING POWER from the CENTRUM out through the tips of your fingers. Step out on your right foot one step forward and a little to the left and turn 1/2 circle leftward. Now swing the HANDBLADES down in a cutting motion, and stop them at the height of your shoulders. As you do, stretch out your left hand first, followed by the right hand. The opponent, standing on your left side, will follow your motion and bend backward.

BACK TURNING

Assume a LEFT OPPOSING-OBLIQUE STANCE. When your wrists are grasped, swing up both HANDBLADES while turning 180° rightward pivoting on your left foot, keep on turning your body in the same direction (TENKAI). Swing down your HANDBLADES and stop them at the height of your shoulders as you stretch out your right hand. Your opponent will bend backward just as in FRONT TURNING, above.

LEFT TURNING

Assume a LEFT OPPOSING OBLIQUE STANCE, draw your left foot back about 270° to the left, pivoting on your right foot. Then continue the movement by rotating your axis in the same left-ward direction. Lead the opponent's body from his hands in a smoothly turning motion.

These BOTH HANDS GRASPED BODY TURN-ING movements, where your body is turned on your feet and the opponent follows the movement, thus somewhat stretching his back, become a healthy warm-up exercise. The FOOTWORK may very to some extent, according to your and the opponent's physique. You may also devise other combinations of TAI-SABAKI and ASHI-SABAKI so it is not always imperitive to follow these instructions exactly.

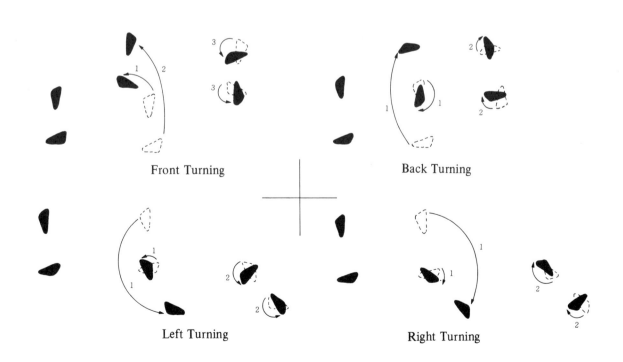

Front Turning

Back Turning

Left Turning

Right Turning

USHIRO-TORI TENKAN-HO
(BEHIND BOTH HANDS GRASPED
BODY TURNING)   [See Photos]

When both your hands are grasped from behind, turn on your left or right foot, reversing your position and your opponent's by getting behind him and gently bending his body backward.

It is not possible to make him follow if your hands, hips and feet do not function in the completely united movement which is the basis of all BODY TURNING.

When you begin turning, put your wrists on your hips with the palms up, put your right foot a step forward and to the right. Extend your HAND-BLADES out to the front and up, at the same screwing them inward. Now step around to your right front with your left foot as if to turn toward your partner and draw back your right foot to complete the exercise at the point where he is bent backwards but has not fallen. This movement is thus a good front body stretch as well.

RENZOKU TENKAN-HO
(CONTINUOUS BODY TURNING)
                             [Not Shown]

This term refers simply to any of the BODY TURNING exercises when repeated in a series. Keep on turning in the same direction and feel yourself as the axis of the opponent's rotation as he grasps your wrists and follows on the circumference of your circular movement. Repeat each body change about three times, both right and left. There are *RENZOKU TENKAN-HO* from *KATATE-TORI, USHIRO RYOTE-TORI, RYO-HIJI-TORI* (BOTH ELBOWS GRASPED) and most other forms of simple grasping.

2. *SHUMATSU DOSA (HAISHIN UNDO)* (AFTER PRACTICE BACK BENDING EXERCISE)

There are few cases of bending over backwards in the movements of Aikido. But in order to make our body flexible, we repeat them as a part of PAIRED EXERCISE at the end of the practice period. With your wrists grasped from the front, swing your HANDBLADES forward and up, EXTENDING POWER through the tips of your hands. Step in and turn 180° rightward, put your back and the opponent's together, slightly squat and put him on your back. Now bend at the waist and draw him backward as your body bends forward. Do not forget that the movement of your hands and feet should be harmonized with that of your body even in this sort of exercise.

3. *KOKYU-RYOKU NO YOSEI-HO* (BREATH POWER DEVELOPMENT EXERCISE) [See Bottom Photo Series]

In Aikido, we often use and here expressions like *KI* (the VITAL FORCE), *KI NO CHIKARA* (KI POWER), or *KI NO NAGARE* (the FLOW OF KI). During the execution of Aikido techniques, if *Ki* is utilized as the essence of every movement, it is called *KOKYU-RYOKU* (BREATH POWER). No Aikido techniques can be properly executed without BREATH POWER.

ZA-GI KOKYU-HO (SEATED BREATH POWER EXERCISE)

This exercise begins with sitting in *SEIZA*. The basic form could be described as *SUWARI-WAZA, RYOTE-TORI KOKYU-HO* (SEATED TECHNIQUE, BOTH HANDS GRASPED BREATH POWER EXERCISE). Here the opponent sits opposite you and grasps both your wrist naturally from the outside.

When your wrists are grasped, push your hands toward his shoulders in a relaxed manner, screwing them inward with your BREATH POWER flowing out from the tips of your fingers. Fell his body leftward or rightward by stretching out your left or right hand, and turning to face him again as you follow through by pinning him with full BREATH POWER. This exercise is slightly different according to how the opponent has grasped. Some examples are shown at the center of the next page.

ZA-GI KOKYU-HO

One-hand grasped exercise

Various grips

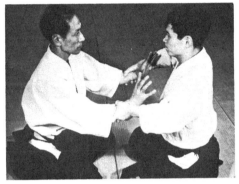
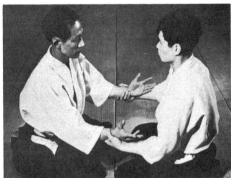

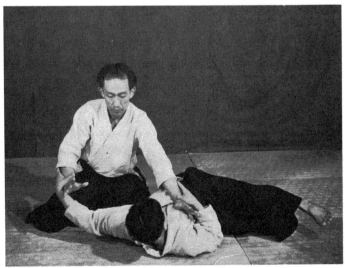

TE-SABAKI
(HANDWORK)

ASHI-SABAKI
(FOOTWORK)

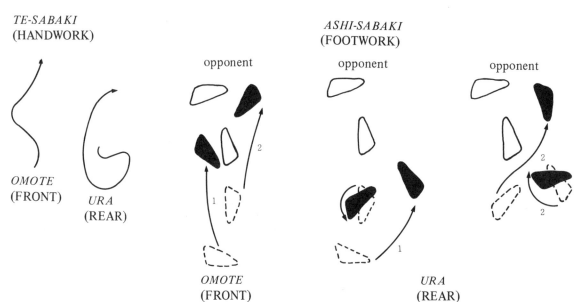

OMOTE
(FRONT)

URA
(REAR)

opponent

opponent

opponent

OMOTE
(FRONT)

URA
(REAR)

TACHI-WAZA, KOKYU-HO (STANDING BREATH POWER EXERCISE)

If you are in an OBLIQUE STANCE and the opponent approaches you from the side and grasps your wrist, you can use either of two STANDING EXERCISES (*TACHI-WAZA*).
OMOTE (FRONT)   [See Photos]
When your right hand is grasped, put your left foot a step forward in front of the opponent's left foot, and step out your right foot behind him. While your body is moving, push up your right hand in front of him, EXTENDING POWER through the tips of your hands. With your hips and knees as a base, turn up your right palm, then cut downward and fell him with both hands.

URA (REAR)   [Not Shown]
When in a RIGHT-OBLIQUE STANCE and your
wrist is grasped, turn your body leftward and
back, pivoting on your forward right foot. Let
your right hand follow your body leftward, extending the arm flexibly. Step in on your right foot
behind the opponent, face him by turning your
hips rightward and fell him with both hands much
the same as in the *OMOTE* form.
These BREATH-POWER EXERCISES vary according to the grip of the opponent. Those explained
above are typical.
If your are in an OBLIQUE STANCE and the opponent approaches you from the side and grasps
your wrist, you can do either of two STANDING
TECHNIQUES (*TACHI-WAZA*). In most Aikido
techniques, an *OMOTE* or FRONT form and an
URA or REAR form are distinguished for the
sake of teaching. *OMOTE-WAZA* may be called
FRONT TECHNIQUES and are generally applied
directly to the opponent from the front and to the
side. *URA-WAZA* or REAR TECHNIQUES are
applied more indirectly usually after entering to
the rear and side of the opponent and often while
rotating to the outside around your vertical axis.
The same distinction can be applied to the *TACHI-*

WAZA KOKYU-HO.
In the BREATH POWER EXERCISES, the SEA-
TED TECHNIQUES (*SUWARI-WAZA*) are the
most important. *ZA-GI KOKYU-HO* is more dif-
ficult than the STANDING TECHNIQUE (*TACHI-
WAZA*). Thus by acquiring skill in *SUWARI-
WAZA* you will be able to master the *TACHI-
WAZA.*
Remember these points:
    1. Avoid a foolish strength contest with the
    opponent.
    2. Move your body in a circular way and your
    hand in a screwing motion so as not to be
    hindered by the opponent's power.
    3. Use the power of your whole body, and do
    not attempt to be clever by only using con-
    centrated spurts of power.
The BREATH-POWER EXERCISE is a special
exercise for Aikido. The depth of your physical
technique and mental state is determined by two
factors: whether or not you have BREATH
POWER, and the degree of its strength. Therefore
KOKYU-HO is most basic in the practice of
Aikido. Constant repetition of the SITTING
EXERCISE, in particular, is the best way to master
the other techniques which follow.

basic techniques
— KIHON WAZA —

OMOTE-WAZA

NAGA WAZA (THROWING TECHNIQUES)

Among the throwing techniques of Aikido, the four which follow are most basic:

1. *SHINHO-NAGE*   3. *KAITEN-NAGE*
2. *IRIMI-NAGE*   4. *KOTE-GAESHI*

1. *SHIHO-NAGE* (FOUR SIDE THROW)

The form of this technique came from Japanese swordsmanship. It involves turning on the left or right foot and "cutting" in any of the four directions. This throw illustrates those typical Aikido movements which are the bodily realization of the rationale of sword use. During practice, while repeating this throw, you will naturally acquire the essential movements and turns of Aikido. Training in this technique is divided into SITTING V. S. STANDING (*HANMI-HANDACHI*) and STANDING TECHNIQUE (*TACHI-WAZA*). The ONE HAND GRASPED FOUR SIDE THROW will be explained here in its standing form.

KATATE-TORI SHIHO-NAGE (ONE HAND GRASPED FOUR SIDE THROW)
OMOTE (FRONT)   [See Photos]
Start from a MUTUAL RIGHT OBLIQUE STANCE (*MIGI AI-HANMI*). When the opponent grasps your left wrist with his right hand, EXTEND POWER through the tips of your left fingers. Grasp his right wrist with your right hand and

at the same time put your right foot right and a little forward. Swing up your left HANDBLADE in a screwing motion as you step out on your left foot to the opponent's left with a deep stride. Now turn your axis 180° rightward and throw him by cutting downward with your HANDBLADE as your right foot moves a step forward to his rear.

URA (REAR)   [Not Shown]
The opponent assumes a RIGHT OBLIQUE STANCE and you a LEFT (*GYAKU-HANMI*). As soon as he grasps your left wrist with his right hand, grasp his right wrist with your right hand, turn back about 180° to the right by pivoting on your left foot. Swing up your left HANDBLADE and execute a *TENKAI* body change on the balls of your feet (movement 3 in the footwork diagram). Now cut down with your HANDBLADES as you step in toward his rear with your inside, right foot for the throw.

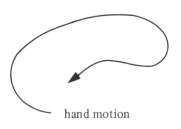

hand motion

ASHI-SABAKI (FOOT WORK)

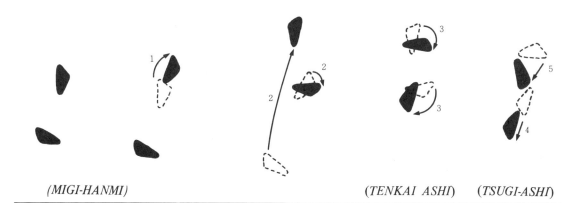

(MIGI-HANMI)   (TENKAI ASHI)   (TSUGI-ASHI)

URA-WAZA

2. *IRIMI-NAGE* (ENTERING THROW)

This is a technique of passing out of the opponent's line of attack. Move away from his power, ENTER to his side, and throw him with the movement of your CENTRUM.

KOSA-TORI IRIMI-NAGE
(DIAGONAL ONE HAND GRASPED ENTERING THROW)

OMOTE (FRONT)   [See Diagrams]
As soon as the opponent grasps the inside of your right wrist with his right hand, step in on your left foot behind his right side and grasp the back of his collar. At the same time, pull back your right hand as if drawing an arc at your waist, stretch out the arc, and unbalance his body forward. Continue to screw your right hand inward and lead his right

hand out and up, matching his instinct to correct his posture. Then, turning your body leftward, enter on your right foot a step to his rear, and with your right hand over his chin, fell him.

URA (REAR)   [See Photos]
Do the same as above. When you grasp the opponent's collar with your left hand, lead his right hand and then unbalance him with your right hand moving in an arc. At this moment, swing your right foot around backward with a *TENKAN*, pivoting to the outside around your left foot, and unbalance him by the speed of your rotating axis and the movement of your CENTRUM. When he resists the forward falling movement by pulling his body backward, reverse your direction, hook him over his chin with your right hand and fell him as you ENTER behind.

OMOTE-WAZA

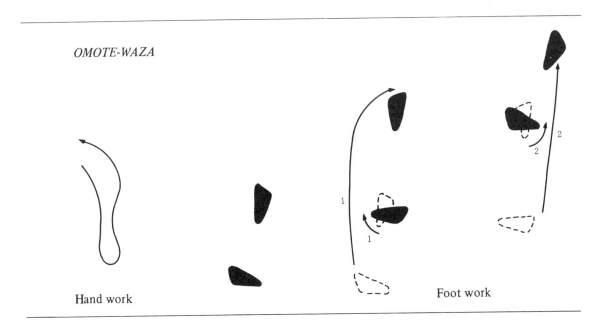

Hand work   Foot work

3. *KAITEN-NAGE* (ROTARY THROW)

The movements of Aikido must always be circular, not angular. This circular movement should never be two-dimensional, but should always be spherical. ROTARY THROW is so named because the opponent rolls forward like a ball when felled. Your body movements become skillful in rotation techniques as well as simple reversal techniques. This is the reason why ROTARY THROW is considered a basic technique.

Aikido is a dynamic art and photos often miss much of this. In the early stages of training you may practice by setting up *MA-AI* (DISTANCE) and moving from static STANCES but the ideal is to take active command of the situation. That means going out to meet the opponent as he comes to attack and inducing him to grasp you as you wish. Here we start in a MUTUAL RIGHT OBLIQUE STANCE and then move into the action seen in the first frame. Throughout the book you may find cases where this is the case.

UCHI KAITEN-NAGE (INSIDE ROTARY THROW)

Move in from a MUTUAL RIGHT OBLIQUE STANCE. As soon as the opponent grasps your left wrist with his right hand, check his face with your right fist, EXTEND POWER and swing up your left HANDBLADE in a screwing motion from below and to the outside of his grasping hand. At the same time your left foot slides half a step to his right front. Then, stepping your right foot to his right rear, pass under your raised arms and turn your axis leftward about half a circle or slightly more. Now pull back your left foot with a deep step and cut downward with your left HANDBLADE in a sweeping arc that follows the movement of your body. Your left shoulder should be the center of this arc and the downward movement should cause his body to bend forward. Use your right hand to suppress his neck when it reaches its lowest point and continue the flowing movement of your left HANDBLADE up and under his right wrist so that his arm is stretched vertically over his head. EXTEND POWER through your left hand and with a motion originating from your hips, roll him forward as your left foot steps forward and your straighten your posture.

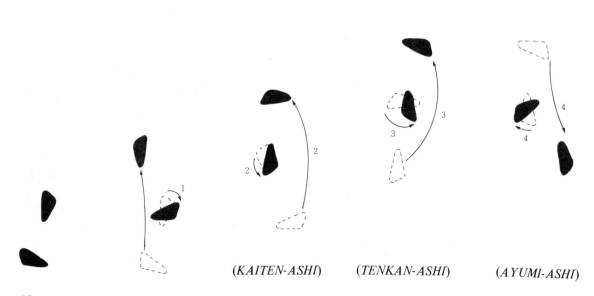

(*KAITEN-ASHI*)   (*TENKAN-ASHI*)   (*AYUMI-ASHI*)

SOTO KAITEN-NAGE
(OUTSIDE ROTARY THROW)

Assume an OPPOSING LEFT OBLIQUE STANCE; that is, you are in LEFT but your opponent is in a RIGHT OBLIQUE STANCE. As soon as the opponent grasps your left wrist, swing up your left HANDBLADE toward the outside (i. e., the back) of his grasping hand in a big arc with your left shoulder as its axis. During this movement move your right foot backward by pivoting 180° on your left foot. Now you are standing side by side. Then while you are pulling your left foot a deep step backward, draw a complete circle downward then up with your left hand which his right hand is still grasping. Suppress his neck with your right hand, put your left foot a step forward and straighten your posture as you roll him forward by the BREATH POWER in your hands.

URA-WAZA

Turning his wrist

4. *KOTE-GAESHI* (WRIST OUT-TURN)

One of the secondary aims of Aikido exercise is to develop a strong body. Hence an effective and natural exercise is needed. If unnatural exercise is repeated, it will cause an, at first, unnoticed but harmful effect on your body.

This joint throw, called WRIST OUT-TURN, is executed in the direction in which the joints will bend naturally.

KOSA-TORI KOTE-GAESHI (DIAGONAL GRASP, WRIST OUT-TURN) [See Photos]

Start from MUTUAL RIGHT OBLIQUE STANCE with the opponent taking your right hand with his right in *KOSA-TORI* fashion. As the opponent attacks, step in to his right rear on your left foot. Then open rightward and let your right hand, which he is coming to take, follow your body in a big arc as your right leg swings around to your rear. As you unbalance his body with this movement, take hold of his right hand with your left hand. Be sure to place your thumb on the back of his hand and your fingers over his palm at the root of his thumb. Now TURN back leftward on your right foot while you put your right hand on the back of his right to support your left thumb in turning his wrist out to your left. Throw him as if your were rolling him up in a rug. When the starting stances are reversed the movements will all be reversed.

SHOMEN-UCHI (FRONTAL STRIKE)

KATAME WAZA (OSAE WAZA) (LOCKING AND PINNING TECHNIQUES)

The techniques of Aikido consist of THROWING TECHNIQUES and LOCKING AND PINNING TECHNIQUES. The latter are especially refined and exquisite because Master Ueshiba Morihei's Aikido developed out of his study of *jujutsu,* the old Japanese self-defense arts. Locks and pins are used only after you throw, fell, or strike (*ATEMI*) the opponent, and result in a face-down pin that will render him helpless with little effort on your part.

If the opponent is skillful in falling, it is possible that he will not be incapacitated when thrown and may get up to attack again. The significance and importance of pinning is that this kind of response can be prevented.

1. *IKKYO UDE-OSAE* (ARM PIN)

The ARM PIN is the most important of these four basic techniques. In Aikido it is said that you hardly need to learn the other techniques if you completely master *IKKYO.*

BREATH POWER, ENTERING, punching, and especially the harmonious movement of hips and knees, are completely coordinated in this move. In earlier days this was the first movement to be learned by beginners. Hence it is called *ikkyo—* the "First Teaching."

SHOMEN-UCHI IKKYO

OMOTE-WAZA

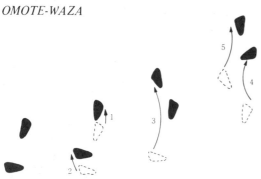

SHOMEN-UCHI IKKYO UDE-OSAE (FRONTAL STRIKE ARM PIN)

OMOTE (FRONT) [See Photos]

Assume a MUTUAL RIGHT OBLIQUE STANCE. Put your right HANDBLADE up with enough BREATH POWER to check the opponent's overhead attack as your right foot slides half a step forward and to the right, taking you off the line of attack. At the same time your left hand thrusts out as if to strike his exposed ribs and continues up to grasp his right arm just below the elbow. Now your right cuts down his right arm in concert with your left hand at his elbow and you grasp his right wrist from the pulse side with your right hand. Step in to his front on your left foot and then step diagonally to the right on your right foot and pin him.

Note:
- Don't be passive when you are first facing the opponent.
- Don't grasp the opponent's arm rigidly Extend your hands flexibly, basing all movements on your hips.
- Stretch out the opponent's arm. Pin it at a position higher than his shoulder line. Don't pin with arm power. Pin with your BREATH POWER flowing from your CENTRUM. Be prepared for other opponents on all four sides.

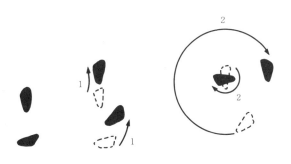

URA (REAR)   [See Photos Below]

Assume a LEFT OPPOSING OBLIQUE STANCE. As he attacks, ENTER and TURN about 270 degrees back to your right around your left foot. Cut down his attack with your HANDBLADE while you turn your body. Grasp and pin him as in *OMOTE*.

If unreasonable FORCE is used in trying to pull him downward, you will be unbalanced immediately. Therefore it is necessary to turn with your hands EXTENDED, out from your body, in an elastic and flexible fashion.

URA-WAZA

2. NIKYO KOTE-MAWASHI (WRIST IN-TURN)

WRIST IN-TURN or *NIKYO*, the "Second Teaching," is an exercise of wrist, elbow and shoulder joints. It will be a shock to your wrist joints until you become accustomed to it. Your joints will become strengthened in a short time because this exercise is based on natural joint-bending principles.

SHOMEN-UCHI NIKYO KOTE-MAWASHI (FRONTAL STRIKE WRIST IN-TURN)

OMOTE (FRONT)   [See Photos, Next Page]

Check the opponent as in *IKKYO* and immediately put your left foot a step in front of him as you cut down his attack and break his posture. Slide your right palm around the back of his right hand so as to turn his right wrist forward and enable you to grasp the hand from the back. All the while, your left hand must push his body forward from the inside of his elbow region to prevent him from recovering his balance. Now step diagonally forward with your right foot, turning rightward at your hips and bring him to the mats. Face his fallen body and sit down onto the balls of your feet (*KIZA*). Move his right wrist over to your left elbow and pinch it there tightly to your chest, at the same time maintaining the torsion on his elbow with your left HANDBLADE. Now change and let your right hand take over the control of his elbow and turn his right arm toward his head using a twisting movement of your hips and upper body.

Note:

- When turning your wrist and grasping the back of the opponent's hand, base your action on balanced hips.
- When you loosen the grasp of your right hand to pin, put spirited concentration in your left hand to check his counter attack.
- When PINNING, check his shoulder from above with your right knee and check his ribs with your left knee. Pin him with a relaxed upper body. As the opponent cannot move when pinned in this way, don't give your attention only to him.
- Be prepared for other opponents.

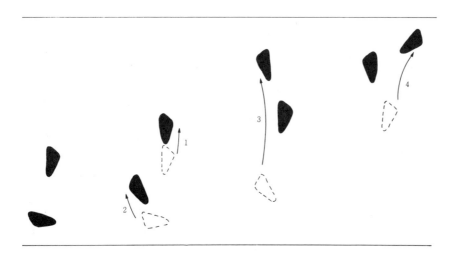

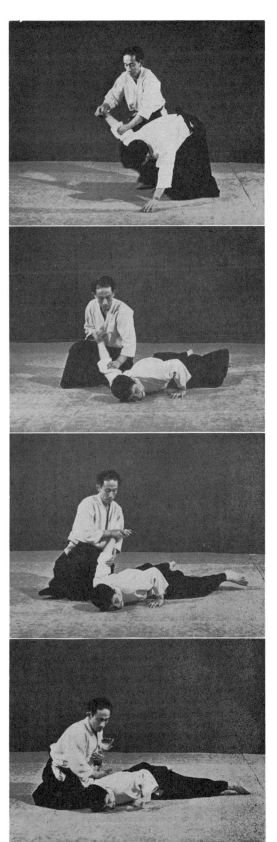

SHOMEN-UCHI NIKYO KOTE-MAWASHI URA-WAZA

1	2	3	4
5			
6	7	8	9

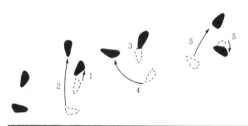

URA (REAR)   [See Photos]

ENTER and TURN on your ledt foot about 90
degrees backward as your hands cut down his
attacking arm as in *OMOTE*. Tightly hold down
the elbow with your left hand and turn his right
wrist rightward with your right hand while you
are opening your body. Now pin the turned wrist
firmly to the front of your left shoulder, thumb
down. To do this, slide your left hand from his
elbow to his wrist, somewhat reaching around his
arm, grasp and press his kinked wrist forward with
a movement based on your hips. Pinning is the
same as in *OMOTE*.
Note:

■ Never hold the opponent's joints while

in front of him or your body will be open
to his attack. Be sure to get to his side,
keep a superior position, and then take
hold.

■ As this is a LOCK and PIN TECHNIQUE,
it is necessary to reduce the opponent's
fighting capacity by a thrust or other striking *ATEMI* before executing this action.

■ When moving from the lock to the pin,
twist your right hand forward and right
and press your left hand downward
mobilizing his elbow. Always execute your
movements from the hip region and
EXTEND POWER.

3. SANKYO KOTE-HINERI (WRIST TWIST)

WRIST TWIST or *SANKYO*, "Third Teaching," is a technique which exercises the wrist and elbow joints. This is also based on the technique of IKKYO, ARM PIN, and consists of joint movements and arm pinning. The most typical movements are FRONTAL STRIKE and ONE HAND GRASPED WRIST TWIST. The former will be explained.

SHOMEN-UCHI SANKYO KOTE-HINERI (FRONTAL STRIKE WRIST TWIST)

OMOTE (FRONT)   [See Photos]

Check the opponent's overhead attack as in *IKKYO* and step into his front on your left foot and cut down his arm. Suppress his right elbow joint firmly with your left hand and slide your right hand toward the tips of his fingers. Grasp them tightly with your palm on the root of his right little finger and twist the hand up and to their front-right to lock up his joints. Now, without weakening the lock, bring up your left hand and tightly grasp the back of his hand, placing your thumb on the root of his thumb. Then further twist and lock the arm by extending it toward his head. Cut down his whole body by means of his arm and step directly in front of him on

SHOMEN-UCHI SANKYO KOTE-HINERI, OMOTE-WAZA

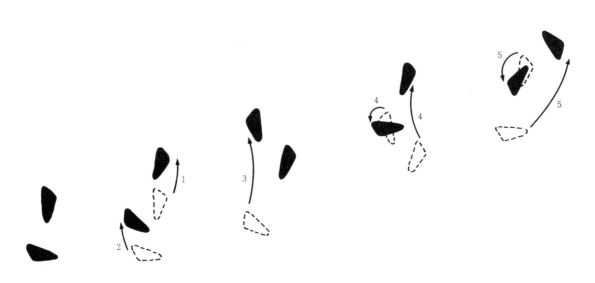

your right foot, suppress his right elbow joint with your right hand from above and turn your body to your left by drawing back your left leg. Bring him to the mats and face him from the right and finish.

Note:

- It is important to execute this form with a continuous movement, always EX-TENDING POWER no matter how slow or unskillful you may be at first.
- When twisting, don't try to check the opponent only with your hand power. Check him with EXTENDED POWER flowing from your CENTRUM.

URA (REAR)   [Not Shown]

TURN your body, checking the opponent as explained in *IKKYO* and *NIKYO URA*. Move to his side, and perform the above technique from the side position, turn back and pin to his rear.

SANKYO is often applied in self-defense situations, walking a drunkard to a police station, or pinning a disorderly person; however its main object is training, like all the others.

It should be remembered that it is important not to put your main concentration on whether or not you are successfully executing the technique, but rather to concentrate on the *essence* of the technique.

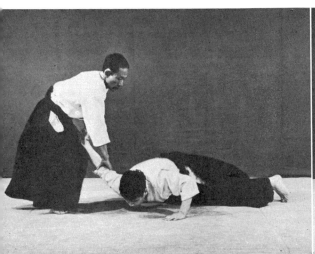 

4. YONKYO TEKUBI-OSAE (WRIST PIN)

WRIST PIN or *YONKYO,* "Fourth Teaching," is the exercise which causes the most pain of all the techniques of Aikido, including the other pins. The exercised parts will rapidly grow stronger however, and the technique will become easy to use in a relatively short time in comparison to your other progress. It is one of the techniques which attacks the opponent's weak points in order to control him.

SHOMEN-UCHI YONKYO TEKUBI-OSAE (FRONTAL STRIKE WRIST PIN)

OMOTE (FRONT)   [See Photos]
Check the opponent as in *IKKYO,* put your left foot a step to his front and cut down his arm. Grasp his right wrist with your right hand, and above your right hand, grasp with your left hand so that the root of your left forefinger will be on his right pulse.

EXTEND POWER from your CENTRUM, basing your movement on your hips and extending out through your hands, especially from your left little finger and the root of the forefinger. Use this grip to push his face to the mats in a spiraling action which continues into the pin from a standing posture.

Note:

- It is necessary to reduce the opponent's fighting capacity by thrusting or striking him at the instant of his attack before applying this sort of PINNING TECH-NIQUE.

- When pinning, it is necessary to flexibly extend your hands, particularly your left wrist.
- Don't forget that in pinning the opponent's wrist the movement should be based at your hips.
- Don't allow your attention to focus only on the opponent. Be attentive of others.

URA (REAR)   [Not Shown]
TURN rightward on your left foot as explained in *IKKYO* and *NIKYO.* Cut down his arm and put the root of your left forefinger on the bone (thumb side) of his right wrist, support this with your right hand, suppress him back to your right EXTENDING POWER and basing the movement on your hips.

YONKYO practice will turn into a power contest if you're not careful. But it loses its value as a technique if the upper body becomes stiff and you use only FORCE. Therefore it is important to keep a proper and flexible posture and not to concentrate solely on one hand of the opponent.

All these LOCKING AND PINNING TECH-NIQUES have been illustrated from a MUTUAL RIGHT OBLIQUE STANCE. Right and left, of course are reversed in the case of LEFT OBLIQUE STANCE. Repeated exercise of *IKKYO* in parti-cular should not be neglected. *NIKYO, SANKYO* and *YONKYO* are all variations of the "FIRST TEACHING," *IKKYO.* They are only slightly different ways of controlling the joints of the arm.

SHOMEN-UCHI YONKYO TEKUBI OSAE
OMOTE-WAZA

applied techniques
— OYO WAZA —

All these techniques are used while standing. They may also be applied while SEATED (*SUWARI-WAZA*) and from SITTING v.s. STANDING (*HANMI-HANDACHI*). In addition, all Aikido techniques are effective in EMPTY HAND V.S. WEAPONS application and in WEAPON V.S. WEAPON situations. A few examples of each category are shown below.

EMPTY HAND APPLICATIONS (continued)

AI-HANMI (MUTUAL OBLIQUE STANCE)

EMPTY HAND APPLICATIONS

Mastering Aikido means to express the rhythmic harmony of Nature in the human body. Its smooth and rhythmic motion is beauty itself. It is dynamic. EMPTY HAND training is most important when expressing this aspect of Aikido. If it is thoroughly practiced, EMPTY HAND V.S. WEAPON training will be acquired as a natural consequence. It is hoped, therefore, that you will study EMPTY HAND TECHNIQUE to the extent that you become able to utilize and apply it at will.

YOKOMEN-UCHI SHIHO-NAGE OMOTE-WAZA

Grasping the wrist

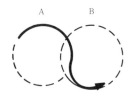

NAGE WAZA
(THROWING TECHNIQUES)

1. APPLIED *SHIHO-NAGE*
(FOUR-SIDE THROW)

YOKOMEN-UCHI SHIHO-NAGE
(OBLIQUE STRIKE FOUR-SIDE
THROW) [See Photos]

Start from MUTUAL LEFT OBLIQUE STANCE. When the opponent attacks with an OBLIQUE STRIKE, pivot on your right foot, moving your left foot back around about one step. Simultaneously hit his face with your right fist or HANDBLADE and use your left to divert his striking hand from the inside of his wrist, directing it back past your left side. (That is, to a point which was at the right rear of your original position.) Cutting his hand down, grasp his wrist with your hands, somewhat twisting it to your right.

Then shift your right foot a little to the right and stride out on your left foot to your right-front, swinging up your hands in a large motion. PIVOT 180° rightward, your weight on your left foot and cut downward with your hands as your right foot steps in to his rear.

Note:

- In an OBLIQUE STRIKE, the opponent's hand draws a circle around his front foot. Accelerate his movement in his circle, and as long as your CENTRUM is stable his action will be drawn into your circle. If we refer to the above diagram, he will lose his balance just as the movement of Circle A is taken into Circle B.

- All the movements in this technique should be circular. Grasp his right wrist with your right hand in a circular motion.

The flow of the hands

√KATA-TORI SHIHO-NAGE
(ONE SHOULDER GRASPED
FOURSIDE THROW)

As soon as the opponent grasps your right shoulder with his left hand, hit his face with your right fist and thrust at the right side of his rib cage with your left. As he blocks your right hand with his right, pivot back to the left around your right foot. Make use of his resistance to your punch to his face to lead his hand back and down to the right of your original position. Grasp his right wrist with your hands and slightly twist it rightward. Now turn your hips rightward and advance, putting your right foot forward to your right and then striding deeply in on your left.

Swing up your HANDBLADES as you move. PIVOT rightward 180° and then cut down his right arm as you step in to his rear on your right foot and throw him.

Note:

- These movements are the same as OBLIQUE STRIKE FOUR-SIDE THROW.
- Because the opponent is holding your shoulder, it is difficult to pass under his hand. So it is necessary to have a stable CENTRUM and raise his body, making use of his centripetal force.

MUNE-TORI SHIHO-NAGE
(GRASPED LOWER LAPEL FOUR-SIDE THROW)

In case your lower lapel is grasped by the opponent's right hand, hit his face with your right hand, grasp his right wrist with your left hand at the same time as you slide your left foot back and slightly right. Grasp his right wrist with your right hand (together with your left hand), pass your head under his right hand and arm moving from the left, and stride out your left foot forward and to the right. Then PIVOT 180° rightward, cut his right hand downward and fell him.

Note:

- The movement of the hands and feet are the same as OBLIQUE STRIKE FOUR-SIDE THROW.
- When passing your head under his grasping hand, it will easily come off your lapel as his arm is "carried" on your shoulder. This movement will be very difficult, however, if you don't first hit his face at the start.

(MIGI-HANMI)   *(TENKAI-ASHI)*   *(TSUGI-ASHI)*

USHIRO RYOTE-TORI SHIHO-NAGE (BEHIND: BOTH HANDS GRASPED FOUR SIDE THROW)

[See Photos]

When your hands are grasped from behind, relax your body, EXTEND POWER from your CENTRUM and put your wrists against your hips, holding your palms up. Then push your hands slightly forward and swing them up, screwing them inward as they rise and moving your left foot a step forward and to the right. PIVOT 180° rightward as you drop your hands down and grasp his right wrist with both your hands. Stride out on your left foot, forward and to your right, and twist his wrist in that same direction. Swing up his hand and PIVOT 180° right again, then throw him by cutting your hands down as you step into his right rear on your right foot.

Note:

- When grasped from behind, regardless of the body part which has been taken, you should settle your power into the CENTRUM, relaxing your upper body and filling yourself with KI, the SPIRITPOWER or VITAL FORCE.
- When grasped at your wrists from behind, loosen the opponent's thumbs, unbalance him and rise his body by swinging up your hands and spiraling the palms inward. This *TE-SABAKI* (HANDWORK) is most important.

2. Applied *IRIMI-NAGE*
(ENTERING THROW)

KATATE-TORI IRIMI-NAGE
(ONE HAND GRASPED ENTERING
THROW)   [See Upper Photos]

When the opponent grasps your left wrist with his right hand from a **OPPOSING OBLIQUE STANCE**, push out your left hand away from him and to your right side with your palm turned up, while pivoting rightward on your left foot about 90°. Grasp his wrist from over the ulna with your right hand, thumb on his pulse, and lead his right hand further off in the direction of your right rear. At the same time, put your left foot a step forward to his right rear, and grasp his neck with your left hand. Now stretch out your right arm in a naturally curved manner, hook it under his chin and spiral upward as he tries to correct his posture. Then enter on your right foot to his rear and cut him downward with your right arm.

Note:

■   When grasping the opponent's wrist, you must put your thumb on his pulse and lead his hand by twisting it outward in an underhand fashion.

MOROTE-TORI IRIMI-NAGE
(TWO-HANDED GRASP ENTERING THROW)
[See Middle Photos]

When the opponent grasps your right wrist with both his hands from an **AI-HANMI** position in front and somewhat to one side of you, enter on your left foot a step into his right rear and suppress the back of his neck with your free left hand. Then move your right foot back around to the right rear (*TENKAN*) following it with your **CENTRUM** in a pivoting motion that brings your right hand with it in a big, downward arc to your rear. His hands are still grasping your forearm. When his body is about to fall forward, reverse your direction on your left foot, put your right foot a step forward to his rear and cut his body down with your right arm.

USHIRO MOROTE-TORI IRIMI-NAGE
(BEHIND: TWO-HANDED GRASP
ENTERING THROW)   [See Lower Photos]

When the opponent grasps your right wrist from behind, pivot on your right foot about 180° leftward, thrust the right hand forward and up with the palm turned up to lead him out to your front. **EXTENDING POWER**, turn the palm to the outside and enter on your left foot a step to his right rear. Use your left hand to grasp the back of his neck and **PIVOT BACKSTEP** on your left foot by moving your right foot back to the right. Your right hand, palm up, will follow the movement of your right foot. When he is about to fall forward, reverse direction on your left foot, step forward to his rear on your right and cut him down. Throw him with a spiraling movement of your right hand as it follows the movement of your body.

Note:

■   As the opponent is grasping your hand, it is necessary to **EXTEND POWER** to a considerable degree in order to move your body and his.

■   The movement of your grasped hand should always be started from your hips.

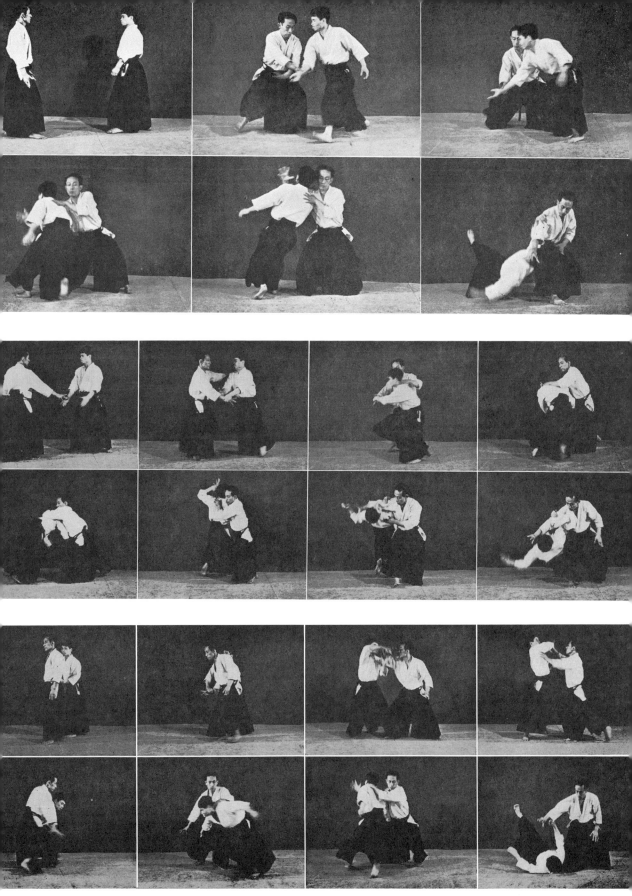

USHIRO RYOTE-TORI IRIMI-NAGE

RYOTE-TORI IRIMI-NAGE
(BOTH HANDS GRASPED ENTERING
THROW) [Not Shown]

When the opponent tries to grasp both your wrists, thrust your left hand across your front to your right in the same line of movement which his hands are already using, and lead his right hand in this direction. At the same time, put your left foot a step forward to his right rear and insert your right HANDBLADE between his right forearm and your left forearm with the palm facing your left hand. Swing your right foot backward, pivoting on your left and continue to lead his right arm further to his front. As you *TENKAN* use your right arm as a sword and cut and rotate your right palm inward as if to make the thumb point down. This will free your left hand to suppress his neck. Unbalance his body with your right hand by drawing an arc at your waist as you pivot back to your right rear; first down, then back up. Now PIVOT back to the left, step in to his rear on your right foot and cut his face downward with your right hand for the throw.

USHIRO RYOTE-TORI IRIMI-NAGE (BEHIND: BOTH HANDS GRASPED ENTERING THROW)   [See Photos]

When the opponent grasps your hands from behind, push your hands forward, palms up, and then screw your arms up and inward. Base this movement on stable hips. Pivot 180° rightward on your right foot by stepping your left foot around to his right front. Simultaneously extend your left hand to his right rear by drawing a big arc from its higher position to a lower one behind his right shoulder. Complete the turn by drawing your right foot back to the right. Follow it with your right HANDBLADE which leads his right hand in an arc down and then up. Now step in on your right foot to his rear and cut him down with your right HANDBLADE.

The Founder Morihei Ueshiba

IRIMI-NAGE

KATA-TORI IRIMI-NAGE
(ONE SHOULDER GRASPED ENTERING THROW)

OMOTE (FRONT)   [Not Shown]

As soon as the opponent grasps your right shoulder with his left hand, hit his face at once with your right fist and his right ribs with your left fist. When he blocks your right with his right hand, make use of his resisting force by stepping to his right rear on your left foot and leading his hand with your right HANDBLADE downward to your right in a cutting fashion. Continue to unbalance his body by suppressing his neck with your left hand. When he tries to recover, step in on your right foot to his rear and cut him down with your right arm moving in a big arc across his face.

Note:

- As this technique is no different from the basic FRONTAL STRIKE or ONE HAND GRASPED ENTERING THROW, forget that you are being held at the shoulder.
- Practice moving your palms and arms so that you can easily lead the opponent with your HANDBLADES.

KATA-TORI IRIMI-NAGE URA-WAZA

URA (REAR)   [See Above Photos]

When the opponent takes hold of your right shoulder with his left hand and strikes or thrusts at your front with his right hand, stop and deflect his right hand with your right HANDBLADE by raising it in an arc toward his face and hit his right side with your left fist. Then pull back your left foot to your rear by pivoting about 180° on your right foot and divert his right hand downward in an arc to your left with your right HAND-BLADE. Step in on your left foot to his right rear, grasp his neck with your left hand and PIVOT BACK STEP again on your left foot by swinging your right foot back to your left rear. Your right hand, meanwhile, continues to lead his right in the direction away from the opponent and un-balances him. Next, reverse direction again and step in with your right foot to his right rear, cutting him down with your right arm across his face.

Note:

- Because you turn your body three times on different axises, your must have adequate stability based on your CENTRUM and knees.
- The power of the hands in induced from the hips — called *KOSHI* in Japanese — the center of balance of the entire body. Hence special care must be taken not to break the harmonious interaction of the hips and the tips of your fingers or your body will lose its balance.

(Also see the note on page 91.)

RYOKATA-TORI IRIMI-NAGE (BOTH SHOULDERS GRASPED ENTERING THROW) [See Upper Photos]

When the opponent grasps your shoulders from a MUTUAL OBLIQUE STANCE (AI-HANMI), form HANDBLADES, step out your right foot in front of and perpendicular to his right foot. Bend forward and duck under his left arm. Step with your left foot to his rear, hook your left TEGATANA under his left arm pit and your right HANDBLADE on his chest, and fell him by cutting upward and then downward.

Note:

- If you try to push your head under his hand, you will fail. Bend forward in a broad move to lead the opponent's body, and then stand up. You will then automatically be under his arm.
- It is important to have harmony and good timing between your moving feet and hips.
- This technique and the next two reveal the close relationship between BREATH POWER EXERCISES (p. 42) and applied Aikido techniques.
They are sometimes considered forms of TACHI-WAZA KOKYU-HO.

USHIRO RYOKATA-TORI IRIMI-NAGE (BEHIND: BOTH SHOULDERS GRASPED ENTERING THROW) [See Middle Photos]

When the opponent grasps your shoulders from behind, back step on your left foot diagonally to his left. Turn your body a little leftward and extend your HANDBLADES to protect your body. Then bend slightly forward and step in on your right foot to his rear and turn your body rightward and cut upward with your HANDBLADES in a large arcing motion. Then cut downward and throw him.

Note:

- If your body is too far from his when entering this technique will not work well. Enter closely to his side.

USHIRO RYOKATA-TORI KAITEN IRIMI-NAGE (BEHIND: BOTH SHOULDERS GRASPED ROTARY ENTERING THROW) [See Lower Photos]

From RIGHT OBLIQUE STANCE, the opponent grasps your shoulders from behind. Raise your HANDBLADES, pivot on your right foot almost a complete circle to the right and cut his right hand from your shoulder with a downward slicing movement of your left TEGATANA. Then draw back your right foot to continue the turn in a sweeping 180° movement. Your TEGATANA should follow this movement and cause his body to nearly fall because his hands are still grasping your shoulders. Then cut him upward, move your left foot into his rear and cut downward with your HANDBLADES as you turn your body back to the left.

Note:

- This is a good example of Aikido's dynamic motion. It shows that as long as your CENTRUM is stable, the opponent will fall.
- Keep your mind on the movements of your HANDBLADES so that they closely accompany the movements of your body.

84

YOKOMEN-UCHI IRIMI-NAGE (OBLIQUE STRIKE ENTERING THROW)

OMOTE (FRONT)   [Not Shown]

The opponent attacks with an OBLIQUE STRIKE using his right hand: move your left foot a step to his right front and hit his right hand and his face with your HANDBLADES. Then catch his right wrist with your HANDBLADES formed in an "X", right hand uppermost, and cut it downward to your right (i. e. to his front) with your right HANDBLADE. Meanwhile, turn your body in the direction of your right hand's movement, entering on your left foot to his right rear, and unbalance his body. Control his neck with your left. The way of throwing is the same as in other *IRIMI-NAGE*.

URA (REAR)   [Not Shown]

Divert the power of the opponent's attacking right hand with your left HANDBLADE, your left foot taking a step to your own left-rear by pivoting on your right foot. Cross your HANDBLADES, move your left foot a step in to his right side and turn your body rightward on your left foot in a sweeping 180° motion to unbalance his body. The throw is the same as before.

In these movements, the evasions are much as in *YOKOMEN-UCHI NIKYO* (p124, 125).

Note:

■ Don't misunderstand that EXTENDING POWER applies only while throwing. Unless you are filled with enough *KI* to get the opponent into your movement, it is impossible to unbalance his body with your body movements.

■ If you don't move your hands carefully, your execution of this technique will be sluggish.

YOKOMEN-UCHI IRIMI-NAGE (OBLIQUE STRIKE ENTERING THROW)

A Flowing Variation of *IRIMI-NAGE URA*

[See Photos]

In this case we do not deflect and reverse the opponent's arm, rather we cut it down once and proceed with it down. When the opponent attacks with a right-handed OBLIQUE STRIKE, pull your left foot to your-rear, pivoting on your right foot. Simultaneously hit his right wrist with your left HANDBLADE and his face with your right hand. Using your left hand, lead his right hand into the movement of your leftward turn. Grasp his right wrist from his ulna side with your right hand, thumb up on his pulse, and lead it rightward. Move your left foot to his right rear, as you suppress the back of his neck with your left hand. Continue smoothly by pivoting on your left foot and moving your right foot backward to further unbalance his body. From here the movements are the same as before.

SHOMEN-TSUKI IRIMI-NAGE (FRONTAL-THRUST ENTERING THROW)

[Not Shown]

This is easiest to understand, for it is simply to ENTER to the opponent's side, passing out of his thrust line. When he comes to thrust with his right fist, ENTER to his right side with your left foot advancing a deep step forward, passing his thrust. Then grasp his neck with your left hand, hit his face with your right hand, enter on your right foot to his rear and fell him. The throwing movements are the same as the others.

Note:

- Get out of his line of attack.
- Don't even think that he will punch you. Just ENTER without thinking of the opponent. You will certainly fail if you fear that he will punch you.

3. Applied *KOTE-GAESHI* (WRIST OUT-TURN)

KATATE-TORI GYAKU KOTE-GAESHI (ONE HAND GRASPED REVERSED WRIST OUT-TURN) [See Lower Photos]

The opponent grasps your right wrist from the outside with his left hand from *GYAKU-HANMI*. Step off the center line slightly to the right, then TURN back 90° on your right foot, as your turn up your right palm to the inside and extend it forward. Grasp the back of his hand by hooking your left fingers on his palm from underneath and tightly apply your thumb to the roots of his ring and little fingers. Now, twist his left hand to his outside and back. Use your right hand to push downward on the back of his hand, helping your left hand. Move your right foot backward and bring him to the mat.

Note:

- This grip is a reverse form of the BASIC WRIST OUT-TURN. For a comparison, see the large photo opposite.

MOROTE-TORI KOTE-GAESHI (TWO-HANDED GRASP WRIST OUT-TURN) [Not Shown]

Your right hand is grasped by both the opponent's hands. EXTEND POWER, and pivot on your right foot by swinging your left foot around backward while your right palm turns up. Divert his grasp toward your left to unbalance him. Continue the unbalancing by TURNING (*TENKAN*) on your left foot simultaneously screwing your right palm inward and cutting it back to the right in harmony with your body movements. Hook your left fingers around his right thumb root and palm with your thumb at the roots of his ring and little fingers. Your right hand (which you have been using to apply *ATEMI*) now takes hold of his right hand to reinforce your left and you pivot back once more on your right foot and throw him as if rolling him up.

Note:

- The balance of your hands and hips is important for EXTENDING POWER in this technique.
- Don't raise your elbow when your wrist is grasped.

KATATE-TORI GYAKU KOTE-GAESHI

KOTE-GAESHI (BASIC WRIST OUT-TURN)

Grasping his hand

USHIRO RYOTE-TORI KOTE-GAESHI (BEHIND: BOTH HANDS GRASPED WRIST OUT-TURN)

A Variation of *KOTE-GAESHI* [See Photo]

When the opponent grasps your wrists from behind, half step your left foot forward and left, with your wrists against your hips. Meanwhile, grasp his left hand over the thumb side with your right hand; pivoting on your left foot, TURN your body rightward in nearly a complete circle. He will loose his grasp as you move. Then twist his left hand inward with your right hand, moving your right foot another step back around your pivot point and cut the back of his left hand down and right with your left hand. This is a "rolling up" type of movement.

Note:

■ When TURNING your body, gather speed explosively, or the opponent will not loosen his grasp. No matter how tight his grasp is, it can be broken if the movements of your hands and hips are executed properly.

KATA-TORI KOTE-GAESHI (ONE SHOULDER GRASPED WRIST OUT-TURN) [See Photos]

When your right shoulder is grasped by the opponent's left hand, hit his face with your right hand and punch at his right ribs with your left hand. When he blocks your right hand with his right hand, lead his resisting power to his front by TURNING back on your right foot as your right hand leads his down in a large arc toward your left side. Your hand must move in accordance with the movement of your body. At the low point in the arc, take hold of his right hand with your left hand over the base of his thumb. Your thumb will be on the back of his hand and your fingers on his palm. TURN again on your right foot, opening backward to the left and throw him with a KOTE-GAESHI powered by your leftward turning body.

Note:

- If your opponent takes the initiative, grasps your shoulder and strikes for your face, you block his strike, incurring a similar resistance to your hand; lead this force and proceed as above. In this case the technique may also be called:

KATA-TORI SHOMEN-UCH KOTE-GAESHI (ONE SHOULDER GRASPED FRONTAL STRIKE WRIST OUT-TURN).

USHIRO ERI-TORI KOTE-GAESHI

USHIRO ERI-TORI KOTE-GAESHI (BEHIND: GRASPED COLLAR WRIST OUT) [See Above Photos]

In case your collar is grasped from behind by the opponent's left hand and his right hand grasps your right wrist, turn your body leftward, moving your left foot backward and left to lead him. Move your right foot back to his left rear in a large motion and raise your head outside his left hand which is still grasping your collar. At the same time take his right hand with your left in a basic *KOTE-GAESHI* style grasp. Apply your WRIST OUT-TURN by extending your left thumb and reinforcing it with your right HANDBLADE cutting down on his hand. Propel your HAND MOVEMENTS (*TE-SABAKI*) by a body PIVOT BACK STEP (*TENKAN*) to the left centered on your right foot. Should you be pushed in this same situation, put your left foot a step forward without resisting and do an about face to the right by TURNING on your left foot in a sweeping motion. Then continue with the same *KOTE-GAESHI* as above.

Note:

- In *KOTE-GAESHI*, as in most Aikido techniques, the movements should be circular and sweeping. The throw is executed when the opponent has been unbalanced by your *TAI-SABAKI* (BODY MOVEMENTS).

SHOMEN-TSUKI KOTE-GAESHI (FRONTAL THRUST WRIST OUT TURN) [Not Shown]

Refer to "ENTERING" (p. 21) and to "ONE HAND GRASPED WRIST OUT TURN" (p.54).

YOKOMEN-UCHI KOTE-GAESHI (OBLIQUE STRIKE WRIST OUT-TURN) [Not Shown]

This is a variation of "OBLIQUE STRIKE FOUR SIDE THROW" (p. 72). When the opponent comes to hit the left side of your face, turn your body leftward, pivoting on your right foot and take his right hand. Then execute a *KOTE-GAESHI* as shown in "ONE SHOULDER GRASPED WRIST OUT-TURN" (p. 91).

USHIRO RYOKATA-TORI KOTE-GAESHI (BEHIND: BOTH SHOULDERS GRASPED WRIST TWIST) [Not Shown]

When both your shoulder are grasped from behind, hold up both your hands with full *KI* power to protect your face as you move your left foot back and slightly to the left, dropping back to his left side. Then draw your right foot back to his left rear and cut down with your TEGATANA in an arc centered on your shoulders and activated from the hips and knees. Using your left hand, take a back-of-the-wrist grasp on his right hand which is still gripping your right shoulder. As you do, bring your head up between his arms to correct your posture. Now twist his hand down and to your left with your left hand, reinforced by your right HANDBLADE cutting down on his arm.

Note:

- When moving back, move rapidly to unbalance the opponent's body.
- Here, when you are using the *KOTE-GAESHI* technique, you must cut the opponent's right arm downward with your right TEGATANA because his hand is grasping your shoulder. You may not be able to, or need to put your right hand onto the back of his in such situations, although that is the basic form of the technique (see photo on page 89).

KOSHI-NAGE

4. APPLIED *KOSHI-NAGE* (HIP THROW)

KATA-TORI KOTE-HINERI
KOSHI-NAGE
**(ONE SHOULDER GRASPED
WRIST-TWIST HIP THROW)**

OMOTE (FRONT)

[See Photos Above and Opposite]

As soon as your left shoulder is grasped by the opponent, hit his face with your left HANDBLADE. When he blocks it with his left HANDBLADE, grab it from the back with your right hand moving in an arc in *SANKYO KOTE-HINERI* fashion. Step in on your left foot between his feet, stretch out your right hand, which is now holding his left, in a big arc to your own right as you face that direction. Bend your knees to lower your hips and bend forward about 45 degrees. Roll his body off your lower back and throw him with a harmonious body turning and hip twisting movement.

URA (REAR) [Not Shown]

The rear form is the same as the above except for the initial movement of evasion which is a *TEN-KAN* (PIVOT BACK STEP) as in *KATA-TORI KOTE-GAESHI* (p. 91).

RYOTE-TORI KOSHI-NAGE
(BOTH HANDS GRASPED HIP
THROW)   [See Upper Photos]

Your opponent takes both your wrists from a
MUTUAL LEFT OBLIQUE STANCE (*HIDARI
AI-HANMI*). You counter grip both his wrists
with your forward most hand holding from the
top of his arm and your trailing arm from underneath. Slide your left foot slightly forward in front
of his right foot as you draw your right hand back
to your right and up. Your leading left hand
simultaniously moves rightward across your front
to unbalance him. Now turn your body leftward
with a sharp hip twist and step in on your right

foot to his right front. Continuing the smooth leftward twisting of your body, drop your hips.
Carry him on your lower back from your left
side and roll in his arms to draw him over for
the throw.

URA (REAR)   [Not Shown]
TURN about 270° to the left, pivoting around your
right foot, to unbalance the opponent. Now roll
him into the movement of your hips and lower
back, pick him up and throw him.

USHIRO RYOTE-TORI KOTE-HINERI KOSHI-NAGE
(BEHIND: BOTH HANDS GRASPED WRIST-TWIST HIP THROW)
[See Middle Photos]

When your hands are grasped from behind by the opponent, stick them to the sides of your hips and turn your palms up. Then push them out in an arc up to the height of your face, screwing then inward. Use your right hand to grasp the back of his left hand which is holding your left wrist. Turn your upper body rightward and twist his left hand outward and stretch it to the right. Your feet and hands have remained in the same *HANMI* position but as his body is unbalanced, bend your waist forward, keeping your hips and legs flexible. Carry him onto your lower back from your left and sweep up his feet as your left foot drops back between his legs. Throw him as you twist your body to the left.

This *KOSHI-NAGE* utilizes a *SANKYO* "WRIST TWIST" on his left hand that carries his arm over your head. The important point here is to raise up your hands in a spiraling action forward to facilitate the *SANKYO* and to unbalance the opponent using his left hand as your lever.

Variation:
USHIRO RYOTE-TORI HIJI-GARAMI KOSHI-NAGE
(BEHIND: BOTH HANDS GRASPED ELBOW-ENTWINEMENT HIP THROW)
[See Lower Photos]

When your wrists are grasped from behind, put them on your hips, turn the palms up, then spiral them forward and up. At the same time, step your left foot back to the opponent's left. Turn your left wrist rightward and grasp his left wrist. As your right foot drops back to his left rear, twist his left hand up by extending your left thumb around from underneath his wrist until your thumb is pointing upward. Your right hand now cuts down to grab his right wrist just below the hand. You continue this arc-like movement of the right hand back upward and at the same time cut your left hand down so that his arms are crossed to form a "plus sign" (+) at your right front. Now enter into his right front on your right foot so that your hips contact with his, then pivot leftward by sweeping your left foot back to the left about 180°. Throw him in a HIP THROW activated by your twisting hip section and led by the arm entanglement.

KOTE-HINERI KOSHI-NAGE

RYOTE-TORI TENCHI-NAGE OMOTE-WAZA

5. *TENCHI-NAGE*
(HEAVEN AND EARTH THROW)

RYOTE-TORI TENCHI-NAGE
(BOTH HANDS GRASPED HEAVEN
AND EARTH THROW)

OMOTE (FRONT)   [See Photos]

At the instant that the opponent grasps your
wrists from *MIGI AI-HANMI,* EXTEND POWER
through the tips of the fingers of both hands.
Screw your right hand inward and raise it along
the inside of his left wrist while your left hand
opens him to the outside. Meanwhile, step with
your left foot forward to his right side activating
the effect of your left hand as it extends toward
his right rear. Now step in diagonally to his rear on
your right foot and cut him down, hooking him
under the chin with your right arm and extending
your left arm forward in a spiraling arc from your
left front to his right rear.

URA (REAR)   [Not Shown]

This time when he takes your wrists, PIVOT
BACK STEP on your left foot by drawing your
right foot back around so that your right hand can
lead his left hand to your upper right in a spiraling
flow. Your left hand leads his right much as in the
ONE HAND GRASPED BODY TURNING exer-
cises (p. 35). When you have unbalanced him with
the pivoting, reverse your direction, extend your
hands and arms, one up and one down in standard
TENCHI-NAGE fashion, step in to his right rear
with your right foot, and cut him down for the
throw. Of course the mirror image movements
would be applied from *HIDARI AI-HANMI.*

USHIRO RYOTE-TORI JUJI-GARAMI

USHIRO KUBI-TORI JUJI-GARAMI

6. Applied *JUJI-GARAMI* (CROSS-SHAPED ENTANGLEMENT)

"*JUJI*" means the character for the number ten in Japanese, a shape that looks exactly like a plus sign (+). Thus some have come to call this technique by the nickname 'NUMBER TEN THROW,' or *JUJI-NAGE*.

USHIRO RYOTE-TORI JUJI-GARAMI (BEHIND: BOTH HANDS GRASPED CROSS-SHAPED ENTANGLEMENT)
[See Upper Photos]

When your wrists are grasped from behind raise your HANDBLADES as usual and drop back to his left rear. Now with your outside hand still in a high position and your inside hand cutting downward, you take hold of his wrists much as explained in the *HIJI-GARAMI* on page 97. (You are now essentially holding each other's wrists.) Cross his arms as you correct your posture and step forward to his front, extending your arms forward and down to effect the throw.

USHIRO KUBI-TORI JUJI-GARAMI (BEHIND: GRASPED NECK CROSS-SHAPED ENTANGLEMENT)
[See Lower Photos]

Respond as usual to this situation, planting your left wrist to your hip, palm up, and then spiraling it upward and forward as you drop back on your left foot to his rear. Now draw your right foot back in a large stride, cut down your right arm and open your body slightly to the right so that you can take hold of his wrists in the *JUJI-GARAMI* fashion explained earlier. Now raise your right hand and lower your left to form the CROSS SHAPE that applies pressure to his left elbow, breaking his posture further. Use this opportunity to step forward on your right foot and throw as your arms cut downward.

7. *AIKI OTOSHI* (AIKI DROP)

USHIRO RYOKATA-TORI AIKI OTOSHI (BEHIND: BOTH SHOULDERS GRASPED AIKI DROP)

OMOTE (FRONT) [See Photos]

When your shoulders are grasped and pulled, relax and EXTEND POWER in your whole body. Move your left foot backward to his left and turn your body leftward. Then move your right foot backward-right to his rear as you pivot, your body turning rightward. Cut his legs at a place a little higher than the knees with your right HAND-BLADE, and suppress the side of his left leg with your left hand. Now sweep up his legs with your arms as your body twists back leftward; lift his body. Drop him as you twist back to the right. It is important here that your hands, in following your body movement, EXTEND POWER and spiral up from underneath.

URA (REAR) [Not shown]

When your shoulders are grasped and pushed from behind; TURN around your left foot by moving your right foot forward in a large stride with your body turning leftward. Then move your right foot to his rear and grasp him as your body twists rightward. The rest of this movement is the same as above.

Doshu Kisshomaru Ueshiba; *IRIMI-NAGE*

8. SUMI-OTOSHI
(CORNER DROP)

KATATE-TORI SUMI-OTOSHI
(ONE HAND GRASPED CORNER DROP)

OMOTE (FRONT)   [See Photos]
When your left wrist is grasped by the opponent's
right hand, EXTEND POWER through the tips of
your fingers and ENTER your left foot a step diagonally forward to his right side. Stretch out your
left hand fully in the direction of your entry and
sweep up his right foot with your right hand.
His CENTRUM will be unbalance and he will fall.

URA (REAR)   [Not Shown]
When the opponent dashes to grab your left wrist
with his right hand, lead him by a TENKAN
movement as explained in OUTWARD TURNING
body changing exercise (p. 37) of the BASIC
PREPARATORY EXERCISE section. Then draw
back your left foot and reverse your hips, directing
your actions into his right rear and drop him. The
hand movements after the TENKAN are the same.

RYOTE-TORI SUMI-OTOSHI (BOTH HANDS GRASPED CORNER DROP)

OMOTE (FRONT)   [See Photos]

When the opponent grasps your wrists, EXTEND POWER and side step on your left foot forward and diagonally to your left. Extend your arms out and downward to his right rear paralleling the movements of your feet as you turn your body leftward and enter into his right rear on your right foot. He will lose his balance and fall.

URA (REAR)   [Not Shown]

For the *URA* version, first *TENKAN* (PIVOT BACK STEP) then reverse and enter as in *OMOTE*.

KOKYU-NAGE

9. Applied *KOKYU-NAGE* (BREATH THROW)

KATATE-TORI KOKYU-NAGE (ONE HAND GRASPED BREATH THROW) [See Upper Photos]

As soon as the opponent grasps your left hand with his right, turn 180° to the right by pivoting around your left foot. EXTEND POWER throughout this process and move your left HANDBLADE in an up-then-down arc that matches his oncoming movement, takes over, leads and throws. This action adds your EXTENDED POWER to his own momentum and makes use of his arm as a lever to throw him without resistance.

Variation: *KATATE-TORI, UCHI-MAWASHI KOKYU-NAGE* (ONE HAND GRASPED INSIDE-SWING BREATH THROW) [See Top Photos, Next Page]

As the opponent grasps your right wrist, EXTEND POWER and move your *TEGATANA* to the right and up from the outside just behind his wrist so as to jack up his elbow and wrist joints. At the same time *TENKAN* 180° to the left, moving your right HANDBLADE leftward with your body; that is, toward your INSIDE or center line while you are TURNING. Cut down his kinked wrist in an arcing motion for a throw that is in the direction of his original movement. The *TAI-SABAKI* (BODY MOVEMENT) is the same as above but the *TE-SABAKI* (HANDWORK) is different.

KATATE-TORI
KOKYU-NAGE
[See p.107]

RYOTE-TORI
KOKYU-NAGE

RYOKATA-TORI
KOKYU-NAGE

KOSA-TORI KOKYU-NAGE (DIAGONAL ONE HAND GRASPED BREATH THROW) [Not Shown]

When the opponent grasps your right wrist with his right hand it is called *KOSA-TORI*. Put your left foot a step forward to his right side, fill your hands with *KI* and EXTEND POWER from the tips of your fingers. *TENKAN* (PIVOT BACK STEP) on your left foot, drawing your right foot back around to your right. Leading his grasping right hand in the direction of his initial movement, cut down to unbalance and throw him.

RYOTE-TORI KOKYU-NAGE (BOTH HANDS GRASPED BREATH THROW) [See Middle Photos]

At the instant the opponent grasps your wrists, pivot leftward on your right foot drawing your left foot in a sweeping step back. With your left hand, cut his right wrist down and to your left at his palm heel while your other hand cuts down on his forearm in that same direction. It is vital that all hand movements flow in harmony with your evasive BODY CHANGE if you are to throw him.

RYOKATA-TORI KOKYU-NAGE
(BOTH SHOULDERS GRASPED
BREATH THROW)   [See Lower Photos]

Here again we see that you must become able to move actively to meet the attack. Though he intends to take both shoulders the ideal is to be already moving before he can do so.

The opponent comes to take both your shoulders but you counter with strikes (*ATEMI*) to his ribs and face. When he blocks the attack to his face by suppressing your right hand, you PIVOT BACK-STEP to the left and lead his resistance with your right *TEGATANA*. Cut down in a broad arc and throw him to his front.

It is difficult to execute a BREATH THROW at will, because it is necessary to harmonize BREATH POWER, stable BODY MOVEMENT and *KI*. Daily practice and constant training in EXTENDING POWER are absolutely necessary.

10. *AIKI-NAGE* (AIKI THROW)

This is the ultimate level of technique which leads the opponent's *KI*, unbalances and throws him using only BODY MOVEMENT, often without even touching him. It is most difficult to perfect your technique to the point where you can throw the opponent with only one finger or even less; however, in the Aikido state of "no stagnation" where spirit, mind, and body are one, this is possible. Here, style is free and there is no fixed pattern. Such practice is sometimes called *JIYU-WAZA* (FREE TECHNIQUE).

KATAME WAZA (OSAE WAZA)
(LOCKING AND PINNING TECHNIQUES)
1. Applied *IKKYO UDE-OSAE* (ARM PIN)

KATATE-TORI IKKYO UDE-OSAE
(ONE HAND GRASPED ARM PIN)

OMOTE (**FRONT**) [See Photos, Next Page]
When the opponent grasps your right wrist with his left hand, EXTEND POWER and stretch out your right hand, palm facing downward. Move your right foot back and leftward in a large stride to effect a TURN around your left foot and at the same time strike his face with your free left hand. As you open your body to the right and lead him to his front, move your hands in harmony with your evasive body movement, cut down and divert his left arm rightward in an arc to unbalance his body to your right. At the low point in the downward arc, take hold of the back of his left hand with your own left and, with your feet remaining in the same position, reverse your direction of movement by cutting your hips to the left. As you do, raise up his hand in the direction of his shoulder and body. At the same time push his arm up with your right HAND-BLADE moving out toward his left elbow in a twisting fashion and grasp it from below and inside. Now enter on your right foot forward to his left front unbalancing him and cutting him down from his elbow joint. Move your left foot another step, diagonally to your left, and finish the pin by kneeling down over his arm, both feet erect under your hips in *KIZA* fashion (p. 29).

IKKYO UDE-OSAE

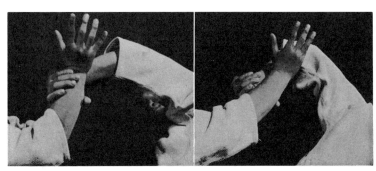

Pushing up his arm

Note:

■ When you first unbalance the opponent's body, remember to have flexible movements, pivoting on your left foot and moving your right hand in a circle.

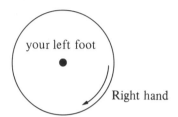

your left foot

Right hand

Circular motion

■ When you attack the opponent's left arm in order to push his elbow joint in the direction of his head, move against his thumb with your right ulna. If you do not execute this technique in this way his body will not be unbalanced (see bottom photos, p.113).

■ When you pin the opponent's left arm, push it forward to slightly more than 90 degrees from the level of his armpit, and he will not be able to move.

■ When you pin the opponent's left arm, twist his left hand rightward, gripping it from the back of his hand with your left hand, and twist his elbow outward to your left with your right HANDBLADE.

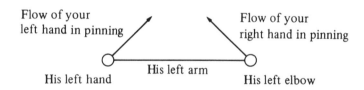

Flow of your left hand in pinning

Flow of your right hand in pinning

His left hand

His left arm

His left elbow

URA (REAR)   [See Photos]

When the opponent takes your right wrist, strike his face with your free hand. Cut his grasping hand downward to his left outside while you step in that same direction on your right foot so as to lead his left hand further to unbalance him. Now suppress and take hold of the back of his left hand with your left (which has just delivered *ATEMI* to his face) and SHUFFLE STEP (*TSUGI-ASHI*) even deeper to his left rear as you raise his left elbow with your right HANDBLADE, just as in *OMOTE*. Now swing your left foot back around about 180° to the left and lead his left arm in a large arc down into the *IKKYO* pin.

USHIRO RYOTE-TORI IKKYO UDE-OSAE
(BEHIND: BOTH HANDS GRASPED HANDS ARM PIN)

OMOTE (FRONT)   [See Photos]
When your wrists are grasped from behind, press
them to your hips, palms turned up, and assume
an OBLIQUE STANCE. At the same time you
move your left foot back and to the opponent's
left. Swing up your HANDBLADES, screwing them
inward, completely EXTENDING POWER through
the tips of your fingers. Move your right foot
backward in a deep motion, swinging down your
hands in a large arc that leads his hands. Immediately suppress his left elbow joint with your right
TEGATANA, screw your left wrist inward and up
from underneath his grip and grasp his left HAND-
BLADE from the back with your left fingers.
Push his left arm, somewhat twisting it, toward
his body center line, and unbalance his body.
Control his left arm with your arms out stretched
in front of your lower abdomen and move your
right foot a step toward his head, then your
left foot another step forward and pin him.

Note:
- If you put your wrists on your hips with
  your palms turned up, swing them up and
  spiral them inward, the opponent's thumbs
  will be loosened; his body will be raised
  and unbalanced.
- When you grasp the back of the opponent's
  left hand from above as your body is rising,
  depress his left elbow joint with your right
  hand and raise his hand in a circle using
  the unrising elbow joint as the fulcrum of
  movement.
- EXTENDING POWER from your CEN-
  TRUM through your body, and out the
  tips of your fingers is always necessary in
  any technique.

URA (REAR)   [Not Shown]
TURN 270° on your right foot, swinging up
your hands as described above and move
your left foot forward and around in a
large motion. Next, cut down your arms as you
complete your turn, and take an IKKYO grip.
Now move your left foot back and to the left for a
pin to his rear.

KATA-TORI IKKYO OMOTE

KATA-TORI IKKYO UDE-OSAE (ONE SHOULDER GRASPED ARM PIN) [See Above Photos]

When the opponent grasps your right shoulder with his left hand, use the same movements as explained in ONE HAND GRASPED ARM PIN (p. 112). Remember to take hold of the back of his hand with a large grip. Open your body and cut downward on his grasping hand to draw him forward and off balance to the front. Then activate your left hand from your hips by reversing your direction with a PIVOT of your vertical axis (*TENKAI*). This will put your right shoulder behind his left hand and allow your to push it up with the power of the whole body as your right TEGATANA moves into his elbow to further break his posture. Pin as in basic *IKKYO*.

MUNE-TORI IKKYO UDE-OSAE (GRASPED LOWER LAPEL ARM PIN) [Not Shown]

When the opponent grasps your lower lapel either with one or with both hands, respond in the same way as you would for a *KATATE-TORI IKKYO* (p. 112) or *KATA-TORI IKKYO* but adapt by holding his grasping hand(s) tightly to your chest instead of your shoulder and thus draw him off balance with the power of your whole body. Then reverse, enter and pin as before.

RYOKATA-TORI IKKYO, UDE-OSAE (BOTH SHOULDERS GRASPED ARM PIN) [Not Shown]

When the opponent uses both hands to hold your shoulders, you are free to hit his face with either hand and then can proceed with the ARM PIN to either of his arms in the manner described above for ONE SHOULDER GRASPED ARM PIN.

USHIRO RYOKATA-TORI IKKYO UDE-OSAE
(BEHIND: BOTH SHOULDERS GRASPED ARM PIN)

OMOTE (FRONT)   [Not Shown]

When your shoulders are taken from behind and pulled, swing up your HANDBLADES and utilize the power of his pull to twist your hips to your left and drop back diagonally to his left side. Continue by twisting to the right and cutting downward with your HANDBLADES as you lower your body and draw your right foot back deeply. It is especially important that you protect your balance during this evasive action. Now, swing your body up again so that you raise your head from between his hands, though they may still be holding you at the shoulders. You are now in his "BLIND SPOT" (SHIKAKU) and can grasp his left hand and suppress his elbow as in a basic USHIRO IKKYO (p. 115).

URA (REAR)   [Not Shown]

In this case the opponent grasps and pushes your shoulders from behind. Respond by swinging up your TEGATANA and TURNING to the right around your right foot. Do this by moving your left foot in a very large sweeping motion forward and around to the right utilizing his pushing attack and leading him off balance. Now cut your HANDBLADES down and swoop low with your body by bending your knees so that you can come up between his arms which are still gripping your shoulders. Take hold of his left arm in IKKYO fashion and pin him to his rear (IKKYO URA) by turning again to the left in a sweeping TENKAN.

Notes:

- Pace your body movements with the opponent's speed and find stability in your actions. Don't be unbalanced by his pushing or pulling.
- Of course all the mirror image movements on the opposite sides from those explained in the text are the same. It is necessary to practice all techniques from both right and left sides.

GYAKU-YOKOMEN-UCHI
IKKYO URA

YOKOMEN-UCHI IKKYO UDE-OSAE
(OBLIQUE STRIKE ARM PIN)

OMOTE (FRONT)   [Not Shown]

When the opponent comes to hit the left side of your head or body with his right hand, enter diagonally to his right side on your left foot, open your right foot to the outside so that you are completely off the line of attack. Counter with a right-handed strike to his face while you deflect his attacking arm and hand with your left. Your left hand should twist to the outside as it blocks his arm in a sweeping movement harmonized with your footwork and divert his power outside and to his right. After hitting his face, your right hand continues down his arm and takes hold of his right hand or wrist. Now you reverse the action and push his right arm toward his shoulder and face with both hands, your left moving up to grasp his elbow. Step into him and pin as usual in *IKKYO*.

Note:

- It is important not to directly oppose his oncoming FORCE but to divert it with EXTENDED POWER projected to your HANDBLADE from your CENTRUM.

URA (REAR)   [Not Shown]

The opponent attacks as in *OMOTE*. This time you draw your left foot back around, TURNING on your right foot, moving away from his line of attack and drawing him into your right-handed counter to his face. Your left HANDBLADE diverts his attacking hand and leads his force back to your left rear by cutting it down during your turning movement. In this way you make contact with his force only at one point and only long enough to pick up the initiative and lead it in the direction of your EXTENDED POWER.

Bring your right hand on down his arm and cross it over (or under) your left and use it to raise up his right arm and begin the reverse back toward his face. Your left hand follows your right and picks up his elbow, while the rightward body change of your hips powers both hands out toward his head. Now your left foot steps in behind his right side and you use it as the center of a 180° TURN to the right which continues as your hips PIVOT and your pin him to his rear in a large motion.

GYAKU-YOKOMEN-UCHI IKKYO UDE-OSAE
(BACKHANDED OBLIQUE STRIKE ARM PIN)

OMOTE (FRONT)   [Not Shown]

Should the opponent try to strike your right side or face with his right hand in a backhanded swinging motion beginning from the area of his left shoulder, move in instantly on your right foot to thrust up his elbow from below before the attack has had time to gain momentum. Immediately take hold of his right wrist as well, and move on through his position with your left foot as your hands cut down his arm in the direction of your body movement. Having broken his posture, now step out diagonally to your right for the pin.

URA (REAR)   [See Upper Photos]

When the opponent's attack has already gained power, step in on your left foot to his right side and, moving from your lower left side, divert his

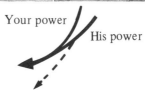

Your power   His power

elbow in an arcing movement, suppressing his right wrist with your right HANDBLADE. Now you find yourselves standing side by side so draw your right foot back to the right, TURNING on your left foot and pin his right arm to his rear in a continuation of your initial arcing movement.

Note:

■ It is most important in checking the opponent's *KI* to move to *SHIKAKU*, his BLIND SPOT. This is a position where he has no way to attack you but from which you are able to attack him at any time. Standing just to his side and a little behind is correct and safe. Unless this ENTERING is done instantly it will be difficult to check the opponent.

SHOMEN-TSUKI IKKYO UDE-OSAE (FRONTAL THRUST ARM PIN)
[See Photos Below]

In Aikido all punches and thrusts from the front including those to the face are treated under *SHOMEN-TSUKI.* The term *MUNE-TSUKI* is used to indicate thrusts to the trunk of the body.

When the opponent thrusts straight at your front, move your right foot around to the back by turning your body rightward in a *TENKAN* movement centered on your left foot. At the same time, suppress his attacking right wrist with your right *TEGATANA* and his right elbow with your left HANDBLADE. Grasp and lead his force out to the right as you move in *TSUGI-ASHI* (p. 27) in that direction. Pin him by suppressing his right arm.

Notes:

■ You should EXTEND POWER and lead the opponent's force faster than his thrust-intention in order to disturb his footwork and throw him off balance.

■ When dodging with your body, don't be swayed with the opponent's thrust, but counter him with a positive mind. Simply imagine that his reason for thrusting is only to be dodged.

■ The movements are easy; however, speed is important in the exercise of this technique.

USHIRO KUBI-SHIME IKKYO UDE-OSAE, OMOTE

USHIRO KUBI-SHIME IKKYO UDE-OSAE
(BEHIND: NECK CHOKE ARM PIN)

OMOTE (FRONT)   [See Photos]

The opponent chokes your neck from behind with his right arm and grasps your left wrist with his left hand. Swing up your HANDBLADES immediately, move your body to his left rear and then cut them downward. Take hold of his left arm and pin it to his front in *IKKYO* fashion. Be calm and *EXTEND POWER* from your *CENTRUM* when he takes the choke hold. Don't harden or stiffen up your upper body.

URA (REAR)   [Not Shown]

Taking the same hold as above, the opponent now pulls you back. Swing up your HANDBLADES and drop back to the left opening your body to the right by TURNING in a sweeping motion around left foot. Immediately cut your HANDBLADES down and take his arm for *IKKYO*. Now *TENKAN* (PIVOT BACK STEP) around your right foot, opening your body to the left and pin him to the rear.

USHIRO ERI-TORI IKKYO UDE-OSAE
(BEHIND: GRASPED COLLAR ARM PIN)

OMOTE (FRONT)   [Not Shown]

When the opponent grasps your collar from behind with his right hand and pulls, move your right foot backward to his right, turning your hips rightward; hit his face with your left hand, making use of his pulling force. Swing up your right HANDBLADE and watch for other opponents who may attack you from other sides. Move your left foot backward to his right-rear, swing down your right hand as you bend your body and raise your head out from behind his right arm which is still grasping your back collar. Grasp his hand from the back with your right fingers hooking on his HANDBLADE, and suppress his right elbow joint with your left HAND-BLADE. Move a step forward on your left foot, and twist his right arm forward with your hands. Then move your right foot a step forward and pin him.

URA (REAR)   [Not Shown]

When the opponent grasps your collar from behind with his right hand and pushes forward, put your left foot a step forward and your right foot forward-right, with your body turning leftward. Hit his face with your left hand making use of his force, and swing up your right HANDBLADE. Then move your left foot back and rightward, turning your body back leftward as you swing down your HANDBLADES. Raise your head outside his right arm at his right-front. Grasp the back of his right hand with your right hand and suppress his right elbow joint with your left hand. Step behind him on your left foot and TURN around it by moving your right foot rightward in a sweeping arc-shaped motion. Suppress and pin his right arm to the rear.

In any case, when you are attacked from behind, combine up-and-down vertical actions with your sideways motion, making use of the spring in your knees and the flex of your hips to get away from his hold. If you do not utilize all these actions well it will be difficult to manage your opponent, especially when he gets over you to apply the choke hold.

Turning his wrist in *NIKYO URA*

2. Applied *NIKYO KOTE-MAWASHI* (WRIST IN-TURN)

KATATE-TORI NIKYO KOTE-MAWASHI (ONE HAND GRASPED WRIST IN-TURN)

OMOTE (FRONT)   [Not Shown]
When the opponent grasps your right wrist with his left hand, suppress his left arm as in *KATATE-TORI IKKYO* (p.112). When his balance is broken, control him with the hand at his elbow and turn his wrist in with the other by grasping his hand from the back and turning it forward and down, toward his head. Using the added twist to his arm afforded by the *NIKYO* grip, pin him to the front much as you would in *IKKYO*. Face his fallen body on your knees in *KIZA* fashion and finish the pin as in basic WRIST IN-TURN (p. 60)

URA (REAR)   [Not Shown]
When the opponent grasps your right wrist with his left hand, hit his face with your left fist and immediately TURN on your left foot by moving your right foot back to your right. Your right hand should lead his left hand to your right so as to unbalance him. After you grasp the back of his left hand with your left, put your right foot a step forward to his left and sweep your left foot leftward and back and face him from his side (a "*SHIKAKU*" or BLIND SPOT). Don't forget to suppress his elbow with your right HANDBLADE as you move into his side. At the same time, twist his left wrist inward and put it onto your right shoulder. Now you slide your right hand up to his left wrist, keeping the spiral pressure on his elbow by holding it under your forearm. Continue twisting his left wrist down and inward (in the direction of your right side) but your hips are turning to the left, a dynamic action that breaks his balance. Now that he has fallen before you, pivot again to his rear and pin in the usual *NIKYO URA* fashion as described on page 63.

RYOTE-TORI NIKYO KOTE-MAWASHI (BOTH HANDS GRASPED WRIST IN-TURN)   [Not Shown]

Refer to the preceeding ONE HAND GRASPED WRIST IN-TURN.

KATA-TORI NIKYO KOTE-MAWASHI (ONE SHOULDER GRASPED WRIST IN-TURN)   [Not Shown]

These movements are the same as ONE HAND GRASPED WRIST IN-TURN. Express your actions with your whole body through your shoulder instead of your wrist.

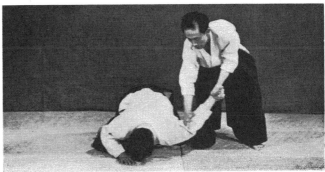

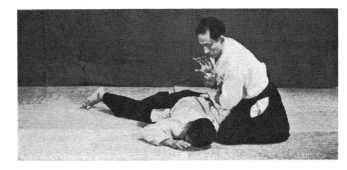

USHIRO RYOKATA-TORI NIKYO KOTE-MAWASHI (BEHIND: BOTH SHOULDERS GRASPED WRIST IN-TURN)

URA (REAR) [See Photos]

When your shoulders are grasped and pushed from behind, move and take the opponent's left arm as in BEHIND: BOTH SHOULDERS GRASPED ARM PIN (p. 117). Move his wrist to your right shoulder with your left and then bring your right hand up from his elbow and use both hands to turn his wrist inward and down. As you do, step forward on your right foot and draw your left foot back and to the right so that the movement of your feet and body take part in the action against his wrist. Keep his left elbow under your right forearm and suppress his arm firmly. Finish with the standard NIKYO pin as shown above.

MUNE-TORI NIKYO, KOTE-MAWASHI (GRASPED LOWER LAPAL WRIST IN-TURN) [Not Shown]

Refer to GRASPED LOWER LAPEL ARM PIN (p. 116) and ONE HAND GRASPED WRIST IN-TURN (p. 122).

YOKOMEN-UCHI NIKYO KOTE-MAWASHI (OBLIQUE STRIKE WRIST IN-TURN)

OMOTE (FRONT) [Not Shown]

When the opponent comes to hit your left front with his right *TEGATANA*, check it as in OB-LIQUE STRIKE ARM PIN (p. 118). Reversing, enter to his front, suppress his right forearm with your right HANDBLADE and his elbow joint with your left, extending them both toward his body and downward. Put your left foot a step in front of him and hold his right arm down in front of your body. His posture should be broken. Use your left hand to maintain pressure on his elbow area as you smoothly alter the grip of your right hand so that the palm is on the back of his right hand. Grasp it and twist it clockwise and toward his head. Now step diagonally forward with your right foot and drop him to the mats as

your hips open to the left. Complete the pin in basic *NIKYO* style (p. 60).

URA (REAR)   [See Photos]

The opponent attacks as above and you lead his power, reverse and break his balance as in OB-LIQUE STRIKE ARM PIN (p. 118). Controlling his right with your right HANDBLADE and his elbow with your left hand, put your left foot a step forward to his right side and TURN to the right 270°. Firmly control and suppress his right elbow as you do, so that your right hand can take hold of the back of his and turn it clockwise in such a way that it further unbalances the opponent's body. Bring the turned wrist to your left shoulder near the end of your pivot, slide your left hand up to his wrist and grasp it, keeping your left forearm over his right forearm. Now lock his wrist with a leftward turn of your hips. Pin as in *NIKYO KOTE-MAWASHI, URA* (p. 63).

USHIRO ERI-TORI NIKYO KOTE-MAWASHI (BEHIND: GRASPED COLLAR WRIST IN-TURN)

Enter into his *SHIKAKU* as in *USHIRO: ERI-TORI IKKYO UDE-OSAE* (p.121) and then put him down with *NIKYO* as described above, either *OMOTE* or *URA*.

3. Applied *SANKYO KOTE-HINERI* (WRIST TWIST)

KOSA-TORI SANKYO KOTE-HINERI (KAITEN HO) (DIAGONAL ONE HAND GRASP WRIST TWIST/ROTARY METHOD/)

OMOTE (FRONT)　　　　　　　[See Photos]

When the opponent grasps your right hand with his right hand, grasp the back of it with your left hand in *SANKYO* fashion as you enter on your left foot to his right and stretch your right hand to his right rear and up. Continue deeper to his BLIND SPOT by stepping in on your right foot so that you pass under his rising right arm. Immediately PIVOT (*TENKAI*) to the right on your vertical axis. Control his right hand with your left and use the power of your pivoting hips to push it toward his shoulder and open his palm as your hips twist further left. Now strongly cut his right hand downward in an arc that causes his head to drop forward and breaks his balance at the waist. Suppress his right elbow with your right *TEGATANA*. Step to his front on your right foot and immediately PIVOT BACK STEP (*TENKAN*) to the left as if to face him as he falls to the mats. Pin him as in basic SANKYO OMOTE.

URA (REAR)　　　　　　　[Not Shown]

When the opponent takes hold as above and plans to step forward, enter to his "SHIKAKU" and control his right hand as in *OMOTE*. When you have the *KOTE-HINERI* grip in place, KAITEN 180° to the left around your forward left foot using this powerful hip action to twist his right palm to the left in the direction of his head. When his body has been driven upward to his rear and his balance is weak, cut his right hand downward in a large arc and take his elbow with your right hand. As you do, TURN back to the right around your left foot, in behind his falling body, and drop him to the mats in an *URA* (REAR) technique. Face his fallen body and pin his right arm without losing the twisting action of the *KOTE-HINERI*.
Note:

- In *OMOTE*, remember to push up the opponent's hand toward his shoulder enough to unbalance his body before you cut it down and step in to his front. Otherwise he may take advantage of your negligence.

RYOTE-TORI SANKYO KOTE-HINERI (BOTH HANDS GRASPED WRIST TWIST)

OMOTE (FRONT) [See Photos]
Respond as in KATATE-TORI IKKYO (p. 112) and unbalance him to his outside front. Use his efforts to correct to ENTER to his front and cut down his arm. Change to *KOTE-HINERI* and pin.

URA (REAR) [Not Shown]
Evade to his left using *TSUGI-ASHI* and apply *IKKYO URA* while making a TENKAN to the left. Change to a *SANKYO* grip, suppressing his elbow, and TURN again back to your rear for the pin.

USHIRO RYOTE-TORI SANKYO KOTE-HINERI (BEHIND: BOTH HANDS GRASPED WRIST TWIST)

OMOTE (FRONT) [Not Shown]
Extend and raise up your HANDBLADES as usual so that his elbows are raised and his CENTRUM is moved forward, then drop back to his SHIKAKU (p. 115). Take the *SANKYO* immediately and pin; or drop him with *IKKYO* and then change your grip for the *SANKYO* pin.

URA (REAR) [Not Shown]
If he pushs, raise your *TEGATANA* (both hands) as you TURN forward to the left. Take his right hand in *SANKYO* fashion. PIVOT your hips and hands to the left toward his shoulder to raise his Centrum. Cut down and pin with a TENKAN to the right.

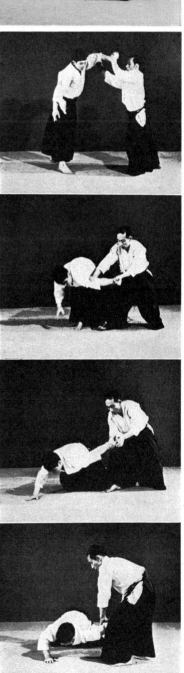

USHIRO RYOKATA-TORI SANKYO KOTE-HINERI
(BEHIND: BOTH SHOULDERS GRASPED WRIST TWIST)

OMOTE (FRONT)   [See Photos]

When the opponent takes both your shoulders from behind, swing up your HANDBLADES and step around to his right front with your left foot. Cut your arms down and flex your knees and hips to effect his balance without your own balance being broken. At the low point of your arc take the back of his left hand and twist it to the right, using the combined power of the *SANKYO* grip, your shoulder and your rotating hips to break it away from your shoulder and extend it toward his face. Now cut his arm down and suppress his elbow with your free hand as you step in to his front on your left foot and pivot around by drawing your right foot back to the right. Pin him face down to his front with the WRIST TWIST.

RYOKATA-TORI SANKYO KOTE-HINERI
(BOTH SHOULDERS GRASPED WRIST TWIST)   [Not Shown]

Refer to *RYOTE-TORI SANKYO* (p.127) but move your HANDBLADES in large arcs and extend power from your shoulders. Or grasp the back of one of his hands and respond with the "ROTARY METHOD" (p.126).

YOKOMEN-UCHI SANKYO KOTE-HINERI
(OBLIQUE STRIKE WRIST TWIST)

OMOTE (FRONT)   [Not Shown]
When the opponent comes to hit your left front area with his right *TEGATANA* move on your left foot a step diagonally to his right front and deflect his attacking arm and hand with your left HANDBLADE as your right foot cuts to the outside, off his line of attack. At the same time strike his face with your right. Now use his resistance to your deflection to cut his right arm across to your right front and downward, your right hand at his wrist and your left controlling his right elbow as in *IKKYO*. Change to the *SANKYO* grip and pin to his front.

URA (REAR)   [See Photos]
When the opponent attacks as above with an OBLIQUE STRIKE, pivot back to your left around your right foot in a sweeping motion that blends with the line of his attacking hand. At the same time deflect his right arm with your left TEGATANA to divert his attack to your rear and counter attack to his face with your right. Reverse the movement and enter on your left foot to his right rear, controlling his arm as in *IKKYO URA*. Changing to a *SANKYO* grip, pivot around your left foot, back to the right, and continue to pivot to his rear and pin.

USHIRO ERI-TORI SANKYO KOTE-HINERI (BEHIND: GRASPED COLLAR WRIST TWIST)

OMOTE (FRONT) [See Photos]

When the opponent grasps your collar with his left hand from behind, swing up your HANDBLADES and drop back to his left side in a balanced and sweeping motion of your left foot and then your right. At the same time, cut down your HAND-BLADES in harmony with a flexible bending of your knees and waist. This expansive movement of your whole body allows you to unbalance him to the front and raise your head up behind his left forearm. Grasp the back of his left hand with your left and twist his left elbow forward with your right. Control him at this point with an OMOTE IKKYO and then apply the SANKYO by smoothly changing your left-handed grip on his wrist to your right without losing the torsion on his arm that keeps his posture broken. Step in to his front and pin him with the SANKYO.

URA (REAR) [Not Shown]

If the opponent attacks from the rear, taking your collar but pushing, swing up your HANDBLADES and move your left foot to your right front to lead his pushing force around to your right while preserving your balance. Now, drop your right foot back to his left rear as you cut down your HANDBLADES so that you can raise your head up from behind his left forearm. As you do, suppress his left arm with an IKKYO activated by your whole body as it corrects its posture. Then enter on your right foot deeper to his left side, TENKAN back to the left and apply a SANKYO for the pin.

USHIRO KUBI-SHIME SANKYO KOTE-HINERI (BEHIND: NECK CHOKE WRIST TWIST)

OMOTE (FRONT)   [Not Shown]

From behind, the opponent takes a choke hold with his right arm and grasps your left with his left. Put your left hand onto the side your hip with the palm facing up, move your left foot back and swing up your left *TEGATANA* by spiraling it inward. Drop your right foot back to enter his BLIND SPOT in a sweeping motion and cut down in a large arc. Take hold of the back of the hand that is grasping your wrist with your free right hand and twist his left arm up toward his shoulder using a *SANKYO* style twist on his wrist. Turn your hands in concert with your hips which rotate toward the opponent based on *TENKAI-ASHI* (p.27). Then cut him down and TURN by swinging your right foot back to your rear to finish with the pin usual for *SANKYO OMOTE.*

URA (REAR)   [Not Shown]

The opponent attacks and chokes as before. Spiral up your left hand as you move your left foot across your front to a point at· your right front side, pivoting around your right foot. Then drop your right foot deeply back to the right and take hold of the back of his left hand with a *SANKYO* grip. Twist his hand and elbow vertically upward from a position below his left shoulder and immediately cut him down and pivot again, back to your left, for the *SANKYO URA* pin.

SHOMEN-TSUKI SANKYO KOTE-HINERI (FRONTAL THRUST WRIST TWIST)

OMOTE (FRONT)   [Not Shown]

When you are in a RIGHT OBLIQUE STANCE and the opponent comes to punch you with his right fist, enter to his left side and deflect his right hand at the wrist with your left *TEGATANA*. Hit his face with your right, then grasp his right hand, push it up to his shoulder reinforced by your left *TEGATANA* at his elbow in *IKKYO* fashion as you turn your axis rightward and cut down. Step in on your left foot and put your left thumb on the back of his right hand with your fingers hooked around the root of his thumb. Move your right foot forward and twist his hand and arm to your upper left by rotating your axis in that direction. Now move your left foot back and leftward, cut down his right arm and pin him to his front.

URA (REAR)   [Not Shown]

Your are in a RIGHT OBLIQUE STANCE and the opponent comes to thrust. Enter in to his right and PIVOT BACKSTEP to your right, controlling his right wrist with your left HANDBLADE. At this point you must be positioned at his side. Now twist his right wrist up with your right hand as explained for *SANKYO* and unbalance him as explained above. TURN back as you cut him down and suppress his elbow with your right *TEGATANA*. Pin him to his rear with continuous movement.

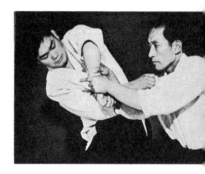

4. Applied *YONKYO TEKUBI-OSAE* (WRIST PIN)

USHIRO RYOKATA-TORI YONKYO TEKUBI-OSAE (KOTE-HINERI-HO) (BEHIND: BOTH SHOULDERS GRASPED WRIST PIN / WRIST TWIST METHOD/)

OMOTE (FRONT) [See Photos]
When the opponent grasps your shoulders from behind, first use your right hand to apply a *SAN-KYO* (WRIST TWIST) to his left wrist as described on page 128. Then grasp his left forearm from the outside with your left hand (as seen in the larger photo found above) and continue the twisting action with that hand while your right moves up and take hold above your left with the root of the index finger on the opponent's out-turned pulse. Now use both hands to cut his arm downward in

an arcing line to the front as you step forward in that direction with your inside, right foot to un-balance and pin him with *YONKYO.*

URA (REAR) [Not Shown]
Move as in *OMOTE* but pin to his rear by TURN-ING back after taking the *YONKYO* grip. Or, move your right foot forward across to your left and lower your body using the spring of your knees and hips. Apply a *SANKYO* (WRIST TWIST) to his right wrist with your left and then grasp his right wrist from the outside with your right to preserve the twisting action. This controls him as you bring your left hand up for the *YONKYO.* Grip with the root of your right index finger against his ulna bone and cut him down with it as you TURN around your left foot by swinging your

right foot back to your left rear. Be sure your cutting action is a large arc that mobilizes his head and breaks his balance. Pin him with a continuous action of the *YONKYO* (WRIST PIN) that flows smoothly from your downward cut and is powered by your turning hips.

Note:

- When you grasp the opponent's wrist and apply *YONKYO*, your hands must move flexibly and in a large arc at all times.
- In *YONKYO OMOTE* (WRIST PIN, FRONT), it is necessary to screw the root of your index finger into his pulse area from the outside toward the inside as if you were cutting into his wrist and downward. In *URA*, put the root of your finger

onto his ulna bone and cut it down toward your center line in an arc that follows your rearward pivoting body.

KATATE-TORI YONKYO TEKUBI-OSAE
(ONE HAND GRASPED WRIST PIN)
Move as in ONE HAND GRASPED ARM PIN (p.112) and pin as in BASIC WRIST PIN (p.66).

RYOTE-TORI YONKYO TEKUBI-OSAE
(BOTH HANDS GRASPED WRIST PIN)
Refer to BOTH HANDS GRASPED ARM PIN (p.112) or WRIST TWIST (p.127) and then BASIC WRIST PIN (p.66).

MUNE-TORI YONKYO TEKUBI-OSAE
(GRASPED LOWER LAPEL WRIST PIN)
Refer to GRASPED LOWER LAPEL ARM PIN (p.117) and BASIC WRIST PIN (p.66).

YOKOMEN-UCHI YONKYO TEKUBI-OSAE
(OBLIQUE STRIKE WRIST PIN)
Refer to OBLIQUE STRIKE WRIST TWIST (p.129) and BASIC WRIST PIN (p.66).

SHOMEN-TSUKI YONKYO TEKUBI-OSAE
(FRONTAL THRUST WRIST PIN)
Refer to FRONTAL THRUST WRIST TWIST (p.131) and BASIC WRIST PIN (p.66).

USHIRO ERI-TORI YONKYO TEKUBI-OSAE
(BEHIND: GRASPED COLLAR WRIST PIN)
Refer to BEHIND GRASPED COLLAR WRIST TWIST (p.130) and BASIC WRIST PIN (p.66).

USHIRO KUBI-SHIME YONKYO TEKUBI-OSAE
(BEHIND: NECK CHOKE WRIST PIN)
Refer to BEHIND: NECK CHOKE ARM PIN (p.121) and BASIC WRIST PIN (p.66).

The above APPLIED LOCKING AND PINNING TECHNIQUES from *IKKYO* to *YONKYO* are all based on *IKKYO*, the BASIC ARM PIN. If this "FIRST TEACHING" is practiced thoroughly, you will be able to use all these techniques to adapt to whatever way your opponent may attack. In all practice, the first step must be a correct OBLIQUE STANCE. These joint exercises are the basis of Aikido training and when practiced earnestly, any weakness of the joints will be overcome in a short time. Then it will be necessary to go further into the various levels of Aikido technique.

EMPTY HAND V.S. WEAPONS APPLICATIONS

EMPTY HAND V.S. WEAPONS APPLICATIONS
are simply extentions of EMPTY HAND techniques. They are the mere addition of a weapon to
your movements. Hence the movements are completely the same as explained in the section on
EMPTY HAND APPLICATIONS. Here representative techniques will be explained.

The Founder, IRIMI-ISSOKU

1. *TANTO-TORI* (KNIFE TAKING)

The following are three posibilities in KNIFE TAKING:

    A. The opponent attacks you with a knife; you are empty-handed.

    B. The empty-handed opponent attacks; you are holding a knife.

    C. The opponent attacks; both of you have knives.

The first is generally considered the typical situation for KNIFE TAKING. It will be explained here.

KATAME WAZA (LOCKING AND PINNING TECHNIQUES)

Applied *GOKYO UDE-NOBASHI* (FIFTH TEACHING, ARM STRETCH)

OMOTE (FRONT)   [See Photos]

When the opponent raises up a knife with his right hand and begins an overhead attack from the front, stride in deeply forward on your left foot and push up and stop his right elbow with your HANDBLADES. Grasp his right elbow with your left hand and take his right wrist with your right hand, your thumb up. Then turning your right hand rightward, step out to his left and cut his right arm downward in front of you. Stretch out and pin his arm. Now take his knife by continuing to stretch his hand out to your right and putting the root of your index finger onto the back of his hand at the base of his thumb. Push it at 90° to the direction of your stretching pin (your right front). When his grip is weakened, the knife can

be easily taken. Another way is to bend the join of his right elbow up by moving his wrist in toward his shoulder until it is under the elbow Then push straight down with your left hand to attack his wrist joint against the mats by means of pressure at his elbow.

URA (REAR)   [Not Shown]

When the opponent attacks you in the same way as explained above in *OMOTE,* push up his right arm then PIVOT BACKSTEP (*TENKAN*) rightward, turning on your left foot in a large motion. Hold and pin in GOKYO fashion, your thumb up, then take the knife in one of the ways previously mentioned.

Note:

    ■ In *OMOTE* and *URA*, when pushing up the opponent's arm with your *TEGATANA,* your *HANMI* STANCE must be positioned outside of the line of attack of his knife or it will be impossible to dodge the blade when it stabs at you.

    ■ Refer to *IKKYO* (ARM PIN), especially from *SHOMEN-UCHI* (FRONTAL ST-RIKE), for details related to this technique.

NAGE WAZA (THROWING TECHNIQUE)

There are two kinds of THROWING TECH-NIQUES. One is simply throwing the opponent and keeping your DISTANCE (*MA-AI*). The other is a combination of THROWING and PINNING. The latter is more effective for KNIFE TAKING. The following is a representative technique.

Applied *KOTE-GAESHI*
(WRIST OUT-TURN)

These movements are basically the same as in *KATATE-TORI KOTE-GAESHI* (p. 54) combined with *IRIMI* (ENTERING) (p. 21). Assume careful distance because the opponent has a knife. Then ENTER instantly as he makes his overhead attack. After the throw, in order to pin him face down, use your left hand to twist the joints of his right arm and wrist rightward so that his palm is facing down toward the mats. At the same time your right TEGATANA should reinforce this action by controlling his elbow from the inside of his arm. Finally, induce him to give up the knife with continued downward pressure on his right wrist. When you are taking the weapon your body must be positioned at right angles to his body.

2. JO-TORI
(STICK TAKING)

There are three possibilities in STICK TAKING:
- A. The opponent attacks you with a stick, you are empty-handed
- B. The empty-handed opponent attacks, you are armed with a stick
- C. The opponent attacks; both of you have sticks.

Here the first two situations will be explain.

KATAME WAZA
(LOCKING AND PINNING TECHNIQUES)

Applied *UDE-HISHIGI*
(ARM SMASHING)

A NIKYO Variation Against a *JO* Attack
The opponent attacks with a *JO* (fighting stick), thrusting from *HIDARI-GAMAE*. *IRIMI* to his outside on your right foot and *TENKAN* to the left, swinging your left foot around deeply. When ENTERING and TURNING, strike his foremost hand with your right HANDBLADE and then grasp it from the back and roll his left hand under your right as you open to the left. Continuing your 180° pivot around your right foot, move his left hand up to your left shoulder and suppress his left elbow with your right elbow. Immediately grasp the back of his left hand with your own left. Now turn your left hand leftward and your right hand to the right in harmony with hip movements directed toward his CENTRUM. This will attack the joints of his left wrist and elbow. The opponent will drop the stick and become unable to move as a result.
This form of *NIKYO* is sometimes termed *HIJI-SHIME* (ELBOW LOCK) and is most often applied against a knife attack.

Applied *KOTE-MAWASHI* (WRIST IN-TURN)

A Variation of NIKYO Using the *JO*

You are using the *JO* in right oblique stance and an opponent attempts to control or take your weapon by grabbing hold of the projecting end with his right hand. At the instant the opponent does so, step in on your right foot moving diagonally to your left front and follow with you left foot to preserve your oblique stance as you move off the center line of his attack. Roll the end of the stick clockwise so as to hook it on the back of his right forearm (ulna). Continue to rotate it in the same direction and slide the end of the stick along his right arm and under his armpit all the way to his back. Step forward on your left foot and then TURN back to the right in a wide motion that reinforces the twisting up of the opponent around the stick. Pin him face down on the ground with the weapon, EXTENDING POWER by means of the *JO*.

NAGE WAZA
(THROWING TECHNIQUES)

Applied *KOKYU-NAGE*
(BREATH THROW)   [See Photos]

A Variation of *KOKYU-NAGE*
Against a *JO Attack*
When the opponent comes thrusting at you put your right foot forward and right and open your body slightly by drawing your left foot back to move off the center line of the attack. Then start to *TENKAN* back to the left with your right foot as the center of the movement and suppress his stick with your left HANDBLADE. When his hands are slightly lifted, grasp the stick with your right hand from below and close your left hand around it from the top as you complete your TURN. Now step on your right foot a little to the front and continue the pivoting action back to your left so that you lead the opponent in the direction of his *JO* attack. In harmony with the motion of your bodies, lower you left hand down and raise and extend your right to unbalance and throw him using the *JO* as a lever.

Applied *SHIHO-NAGE*
(FOUR SIDE THROW)   [Not Shown]

A Variation of *SHIHO-NAGE* Using the *JO*
The movements of the FOUR SIDE THROW as explained in the section on BASIC TECHNIQUES may also be called a "FOUR DIRECTION CUTTING" (*SHIHO-GIRI*) or if repeated at right angles to the first set, "EIGHT DIRECTION CUTTING" (*HAPPO-GIRI*). This particular relationship is the most basic case of the embodiment of the techniques of Japanese swordsmanship which is found in Aikido.

When in a RIGHT OBLIQUE STANCE and holding a *JO*, an opponent may grasp the protruding end of the weapon. When he does, ENTER on your right foot to his front, extending the *JO* so as to disrupt his balance and step in swinging it up as if it were a sword. PIVOT 180° to the outside while he continues to grasp the stick and immediately cut downward and fell him in *SHIHO-NAGE* fashion. These movements are the same as in BASIC *SHIHO-NAGE* (p. 46).

Note:

- Body movements are closely related to stick movements; they must be harmonized.
- When beginning the movement, your leading arm should be grasping the center of the stick.
- Stick movements originated from the art of using the spear. The stick should always move in a versatile, screwing motion.

If these notes are fully understood, not only these few examples but all of the EMPTY HAND techniques of Aikido can be applied to STICK TAKING and also to SWORD TAKING. In daily practices the stick (127cm or 4'2") is easier to handle than a spear (2.7 m to 3.6 m) or a staff (some what over 2 meters).

3. TACHI-TORI (SWORD TAKING)

Practice in SWORD TAKING is limited to two cases;
   A. Sword v.s. sword
   B. Empty hand v.s. sword.
The latter situation is most directly related to Aikido.

KATAME WAZA
(LOCKING AND PINNING
TECHNIQUES)

Applied IKKYO UDE-OSAE
(ARM PIN)

OMOTE (FRONT) [See Photos]
When the opponent comes cutting at your front with an overhead sword attack, dodge his cut by ENTERING to his left. Push up his left arm with your hands, step forward on your right foot from his left side in a wide motion. Cut his left arm downward in front of you with your hands, suppressing his left elbow. Drop him and pin with IKKYO.

URA (REAR) [Not Shown]
The opponent attacks as before. IRIMI and grasp his left arm as in IKKYO URA. Then TURN leftward in a sweeping motion, pivoting on your right foot. Cut down his arm and unbalance him with a harmonious movement of your arms, body and feet. Pin him as in BASIC IKKYO URA (p. 59).

NAGE WAZA
(THROWING TECHNIQUE)

Applied *IRIMI-NAGE*
(ENTERING THROW)

When the opponent attacks, cutting downward from the front, use *TSUGI-ASHI* to put your right foot a step forward to his left while preserving your RIGHT OBLIQUE STANCE. Strike his ribs with your right fist as you move into his left BLIND SPOT and be sure to move your whole body off the center line of his attack. Now step in to his rear on your left foot, simultaneously grasping the back of his collar with your right hand. Moving in behind diagonally, bring your left arm up over his downward cutting arms in the same direction that your body is entering and cut his body down to his right rear with your left HANDBLADE at his chin or face. Entering to the right is also possible and the actions are the same, though mirror images.

*   *   *   *   *   *

When the basics of EMPTY HAND Aikido are mastered, you should be at complete ease in confronting situations of EMPTY HAND V.S. WEAPONS. The difference in any kind of weapons use is that it is necessary to have proper *MA-AI* (DISTANCE). When an inadequate MA-AI is assumed, the consequences are dangerous. Treat the weapon as a part of the body and as the extension of the mind, and there will be no such mistakes. When the fundamentals of Aikido — body techniques — are completely mastered, their basic principles allow you to manage other techniques to counter various other threats; whether from sword, spear, staff, pistol or other weapons.

BIRTH OF AIKIDO

1. PRECEDING ARTS

The Founder's love for *budo* was so strong that in his young days he never failed to visit or invite any man of *budo* who came to his home province and ask them for instruction. His pilgrimages to various traditions of martial arts originated from his driving hunger to know.

The first teacher that the Founder studied under in his teens was Tokusaburo Tozawa of Kito Ryu Jujutsu.

The next was Masakatsu Nakai of the Goto-Ha Yagyu Ryu of Jujutsu who lived in Sakai City at that time. The Founder has said that vestiges of this study are utilized in Aikido hand motion and footwork. He was about twenty when he studied under Nakai.

When he joined the 61st Regiment of the Japanese Army in 1903, his study stopped for a while. He returned from Manchuria after the Russo-Japanese War and was stationed at Hamadera. He again visited Nakai to study during his free time. Nakai was a descendant of the Yagyu family, famous for its sword tradition, and is said to have been a toughly built man, although he was only a little over five feet tall. He was also a man of fine warrior spirit. The Founder obtained a certificate from this *ryu* in July, 1908.

The Founder later obtained a certificate from Sokaku Takeda of the Daito Ryu of Jujutsu in May, 1916. This period of study had a deep relationship with the birth of Aikido, as will be explained later.

Then in 1924 or 1925 the Founder was absorbed in the study of the spear. The author, as a child, felt like crying when he saw his father taking such great pains in his study. He was probing innumerable body changes and motions. It is clear that this became the basis of his movements in using a club, stick, or staff, and also of Aikido ENTERING (IRIMI).

The Founder thoroughly studied old jujutsu, particularly intensely during the period from 1910 to 1925. Had he stayed in any one "ryu" or tradition, Aikido would not have been born, because while Aikido makes use of elements of the old traditions, it is a dynamic part of modern society.

2. THE FOUNDER'S EIGHTY-SIX YEARS OF STUDY

The First Gleam of *Budo* in a Child's Mind

Founder Morihei Ueshiba was born in Tanabe, Kii Province (now known as Wakayama Prefecture), a south-central peninsula of the Japanese main island, in November, 1883.

Until he was 14 or 15 years old, the Founder looked quite weak with his short, thin body, but he was strong and his behavior was quite different from others. He had already had a general interest in *budo* since he was around ten.

When he was just twelve, his father, Yoroku, a member of the local council, was the main caretaker of the village. The so-called Toughs of the town, the hoods of his father's political opponents, would come to his house to negotiate. Sometimes they would rough up his father quite severely. The Founder said that seeing this happen so frequently seared a deep sentiment into his mind. He swore to become strong no matter what it would take, and throw out his father's attackers.

Young Days as a Soldier

In 1901 when he was 18, the Founder took the first steps in the direction of achieving his driving ambition. He had come to Tokyo because he wanted to be a great merchant. He spent busy days working on a wholesale street, and studied jujutsu of the Kito Ryu at night. Sometimes he went to hear political speeches, as well. However, within a few months he developed heart beriberi and had to return home.

On this occasion, he made up his mind to build a strong body and after recovering began walking two and a half miles every day. This continued for ten days. Then twenty. Eventually he began running. He slowly gained physical strength and became capable of lifting two straw bales of rice, while previously he had not been able to lift even one. By the time he was about twenty he began to look quite different. Although he was still short his body was much stronger than ordinary people's. But the Founder was not satisfied only to be strong. He went to Sakai to study Yagyu-Ryu jujutsu. During this time he was involved in fishery and boundary problems of his village, and helped in solving them. Through this work he became well known locally. It was also about this time that he became involved in so many activities that more than once he was a headache for his father.

The Founder was full of youthful vigor. He had an unyielding spirit. If others did twice as much as ordinary people, he would do four times. If others carried 80 pounds, he would carry 160 pounds. His quick temper found good opportunities for expression in the rice-cake-making contests of his village. In these contests a large scoop of a special type of cooked rice is placed in a huge stone morter or bowl. Then a large sledge, something like a wooden mallet with elongated head, is used to pound the cooked rice. An assistant constantly turns the rice over on itself as it is being pounded. Gradually the rice is transformed into a rubber-like substance which is laid out in flat cakes to cool before eating. The weight of the sledge with its awkwardly-shaped elongated head, and the force and frequency of the kneading means that making the cake requires a great deal of strength. In these contests the Founder eagerly matched himself against other strong young men—four, six, then ten. All were defeated. Finally the Founder broke the pounder. He would go to other places to pound rice and again broke many pounders. People eventually had to politely refuse the Founder's offer to help make rice cakes for fear he might break more of them. Instead, they served tea and pastries, in the Japanese way reserved for honored guests, to keep him away from the rice-cake-making area.

When the situation between Russia and Japan became threatening he wanted to become a soldier and joined the Wakayama Regiment. He showed his excellent ability in all stages of physical training, and while only a common-foot soldier, was noticed by the commander of the regiment.

He was only 157 cm tall (5'2"), but he had a tank-like structure and weighed more than 81 kilogram (180 lbs). He played second to no one in his troop when it came to heavy gymnastics, running and carrying. As Japan was at war, training was twice as hard as usual. Many soldiers dropped out. The Founder used to march at the head of the troops carrying two or three persons' heavy equipment. He was considered a valuable man in the battle of Manchuria and prevented a crisis among his troops more than a few times.

Hence when he was discharged from military service he was requested by his officer-in-charge to volunteer for regular service and enter the military academy. He received several visits from his company commander, battalion commander, and regimental commander, all trying to persuade him to reinlist.

Although he refused to enter the academy, he did not want to return to an ordinary life. Therefore the vigorous and spirited young man became a community leader in his village of Tanabe and managed the activities of his district. Kiyoichi Takagi, then just a third grade holder in judo, visited the Founder's home town. The Founder put together a group at the Young Men's Club of the town and had Takagi teach. Takagi later became a judo 9th dan holder. The Founder himself studied judo with great diligence.

But then, perhaps because of the fatigue resulting from his military life, the Founder had to say in bed for about half a year. He suffered from severe headaches and some strange disease. His parents were very worried. Finally, however, he completely recovered. In the spring of 1910, he applied to become a settler in Hokkaido, the northern frontier of Japan at that time. He greatly anticipated the change of air and the opportunity to work in an undeveloped land.

The Founder went to Hokkaido in March of 1911 as leader of a group of pioneers from his area and started developing the land centering around Shirataki, Mombetsu Country, of Kitami Province. Having regained his health and renewed his spirit, and being in his vigorous thirties, he devoted himself to performing his duties. His physical condition improved greatly. He became a horseback rider and would go back and forth in the mountains and fields on business, occasionally braving storms. In this way his heavy training also included developing a resistance to severe cold. Being adventurous in this way, he was elected a member of the council of Kamiyubetsu Village, Shirataki in 1911. He helped and encouraged Mayor Urataro Kaneshige on behalf of the settlers, and was in contact with the Governor's Office of Hokkaido. He organized an association for the realization of the Sekihoku Line, aiming to lay a railroad into the district, and was recommended to preside over the association. His sincere efforts won public approval, and in 1912 the inhabitants of Shirataki (an area about 25 square miles) gave him a full vote of confidence for his activities and respectfully called him the "King of Shirataki."

Caretaker of Settlers

Sokaku Takeda, a master of the Daito Ryu of Jujutsu, was in Hokkaido. At this time the Founder's land development work had made much progress and he had a great desire to study with Takeda.

At the age of 32 he met Master Takeda at the Hotel Hisata in Engaru in 1915 and was told, "You have potentual and exceptional ability. So I will teach you." He became a student.

Daito Ryu Jujutsu has a long history, traditionally claiming to have been started by Prince Sadazumi, the sixth prince of Emperor Seiwa of the ninth century, and has been developed and preserved up to the present. Its theory is deep and the number of its techniques is great. Master Sokaku was quite an expert even though he was short; the Founder had great respect for him. Thus after they met he had an unexpected one-month stay at Hotel Hisata to study with Takeda. Later, in 1916, the Founder invited Takeda to his home, received instruction, and took care of him, including cooking for him and bathing him. The Founder eventually built a new house for his teacher. Takeda was a man of violent spirit and very severe with students who were studying under him. This made no difference to the Founder. He forgot his food and sleep, and concentrated all his energy into their study. This fact has a deep relationship with present-day Aikido.

The Founder's study of the Daito Ryu started in 1915. In 1916 he got the precious certificate signifying his having mastered all his studies. Over that period it was less than one hundred days that he actually studied with Takeda personally. The rest of the time he studied and trained by himself.

For the *budo* he studied at that time he had to pay the teacher three hundred to five hundred yen for each technique (one yen then being equal to about half a dollar). In additon to that, the Founder had to work hard cutting wood and carrying water for his teacher before receiving the lesson. Thus he spent almost all the capital that he had received from his parents.

Serious Illness of His Father

Late in the spring of 1919 the Founder received a telegram telling him that his father was in serious condition. The Founder gave all his property to his teacher Takeda and left Hokkaido.

In Hokkaido, under the guidance of the Founder, the development of land had progressed well. The village was founded, a school had been constructed, and he had gained social prestige and property. But things such as these did not concern him. Only his painfully pleasant and fruitful studies were on his mind. Thus the young Founder returned from the north in the same condition he had gone: with no possessions, save a vigorous spirit.

Study at Ayabe

As he rode the train home he happened to hear of the Rev. Wanisaburo Deguchi the leader of the Omotokyo, a new religion. The Founder, desiring to do anything to heal his father, decided at once to change course for Ayabe, Kyoto Prefecture, where the Omotokyo Headquaters were located, and ask for prayers for the recovery of his father.

Ever since he was a child, the Founder had naturally had an extraordinary interest in the study of spiritual thought and was raised with deep understanding by his parents. When he was seven years old, he studied under Priest Mitsujo Fujimoto of Jizoji Temple, of the Shingon Sect of Buddhism, and at the age of ten he had studied Zen Buddhism at

Homanji Temple in Akitsu Village. Growing older, the Founder's seeking for spiritual food became stronger. He would visit wherever he could and ask for instruction.

The desire for his father's recovery was his main reason for visiting the Rev. Deguchi. However, after having listened to the priest he was struck by his profound insight.

When he arrived at his home in Tanabe, to his sorrow, he learned his father had passed away. Confronted with the death of the person whom he loved most in the world the Founder swore before the grave to break out of his mental deadlock, develop further, and reach for the secret of *budo*.

After that, the daily life of the Founder changed greatly. At times he stood on the top of a rock in a white robe and made pious prayer; or he would kneel somewhere on the top of a mountain, reciting Shinto prayers continuously. His old friends in his village were amazed at this change and worried that he had become mad. Later in 1919 he was attracted with the memory of Deguchi whom he had previously encountered, and moved to Ayabe with his entire family. He sought a light to brighten his heart. A house at the foot of the main shrine mountain in Ayabe became his home. There he taught jujutsu and studied actively under Reverend Deguchi until 1926.

Going to Mongolia with Deguchi

Rev. Deguchi, who advocated a principle of human love and goodness, had an idea to unify the moral world by means of religion. He dreamed of constructing a Peaceful Kingdom in Mongolia with the power of new religions, free from the bondage of old customs, in order to realize the unity and mutual prosperity of the East. Toward this end, Rev. Deguchi had made contact with the Putienchiao religion of Korea and the Taoyiian Hungwantzuhui religion of China. In the early spring of 1924, at an opportune time, he decided to go to Mongolia himself. He invited Masumi Matsumura and the Founder to the Shounkaku Shrine in Ayabe, outlined his program, and asked them to travel with him. At that time Deguchi had been implicated in the 1921 Omotokyo Scandal (for lack of respect to the Emperor), so his departure was in profound secrecy. Most of his confidants were not told about it. Thus Deguchi's party got on a train at Ayabe at 3:28 a.m. February 13, 1924. The Founder joined the party at Tsuruoka and they departed for Manchuria and Mongolia.

Failure of the Attempt

The tentative aim of this party was to reach Mukden and meet Lu

Chan-k'uei, a general of Chang Tso-lin, and then filter into Mongolia with his cooperation.

However, due to the internal problems of China during that time the Deguchi party soon found themselves without help and became wandering fugitives. There were no roads, little food and all they could do was continue to flee from the enemy. During the whole of the five-month trip, the Founder always accompanied Rev. Deguchi and shared his fate. At one point, during a surprise attack by local forces the entire group was captured and robbed of everything they possessed. Even their shoes and clothing were taken. They were put in chains, forced to wear only breech cloths and kept in a prison in Paiyintails for some time. The Founder's manner was somewhat different from the others and his captors immediately sensed he was extraordinary when the group was arrested. Because of this they treated him severally. He was walked in fetters and a pillory. At one point, they were all lead before a firing squad. On the way to the execution ground, the bodies of Lu's forces cluttered the ground, having been shot only moments before. The group did not show fear and strode over the bodies, going calmly to their fate. The Founder, in particular, had an unchanging manner during this critical moment. He was as stable as in his daily life. The others were said to have stared at him in wonder. Fortunately, the intervention of the Japanese consulate at Chenkiatum was able to forestall the sentence and pluck them from the jaws of death. At last, the Japanese government was able to obtain their release and they were repatriated. Arriving at Port Moji on July 25, 1925, they were met by a great crowd which welcomed them as if they had been returning generals.

Though they failed in their original plans, the Founder had had an opportunity to put his daily self-discipline to the test.

Having returned to Ayabe, the Founder devoted himself to his previous life of study and concentrated on learning more deeply the secret of *budo*. The mountains of Ayabe offered an excellent gymnasium for study and practice. The Founder selected a suitable place, hung seven or eight sponge balls in a circle under the trees and with a nine foot practice spear, beautifully thrusted at them in turn. His various skillful movements were engraved on the memories of the students at his side.

At the time of the Founder's return from China, Ayabe was still a lonely country town. Foxes and badgers were seen around his isolated home. Because the facilities of the town were inadequate, the habitants were often asked to donate their labor. As he worked among the laborers the Founder showed his gifted power. Once he pulled out a pine tree which was four or five *sun* in diameter (about 15 cm or 5½ in) and relocated a big stone which more than ten laborers could not move. He would often astonish people in this way. He said, "I taught myself that an extraordinary spiritual power of the soul lies within the human body."

Reaching a New Stage

As his study progressed he developed a type of sixth sense with which he could feel the intended movements of his opponent. When he was traveling in Mongolia he was held up at the point of a Mauser pistol. He became aware of the opponent's intention to shoot because of a small "spiritual bullet" which went through him before the opponent actually pulled the trigger. Then with rapid movement he stepped to the opponent's side a split-second before the gun fired, threw him down and gained possession of the weapon. This is a well-known episode among people who are interested in Aikido.

In spring of 1925 a navy officer, a teacher of kendo, visited the Founder and asked to become his student. Then during a conversation, they happened to disagree over a trifle matter. Tempers rose. They agreed to have a match. The officer dashed forward to strike him, swinging his wooden sword. The Founder dodged his sword very easily each time. The officer finally sat down exhausted without having once touched him. The Founder says he felt the opponent's movements before they were actually executed in the same way as during his time in Mongolia. Resting after this match, the Founder went out into the near-by garden in which there was a persimmon tree. As he was wiping off the perspiration from his face, he was greatly overcome with a feeling which he had never experienced previously. He could neither walk nor sit. He was just rooted to the ground in great astonishment.

The Founder recalls his experience:

> I set my mind on *budo* when I was about 15 and visited teachers of swordsmanship and jujutsu in various provinces. I mastered the secrets of the old traditions, each within a few months. But there was no one to instruct me in the essence of *budo;* the only thing that could satisfy my mind. So I knocked on the gates of various religions but I couldn't get any concrete answers.
>
> Then in the spring of 1925, if I remember correctly, when I was taking a walk in the garden by myself, I felt that the universe suddenly quaked, and that a golden spirit sprang up from the ground, veiled my body, and changed my body into a golden one.

At the same time my mind and body became light. I was able to understand the whispering of the birds, and was clearly aware of the mind of God, the Creator of this universe.

At that moment I was enlightened: the source of *budo* is God's love — the spirit of loving protection for all beings. Endless tears of joy streamed down my cheeks.

Since that time I have grown to feel that the whole earth is my house and the sun, the moon and the stars are all my own things. I had become free from all desire, not only for position, fame and property, but also to be strong. I understood, "*Budo* is not felling the opponent by our force; nor is it a tool to lead the world into destructions with arms. True *budo* is to accept the spirit of the universe, keep the peace of the world, correctly produce, protect and cultivate all beings in Nature." I understood, "The training of *budo* is to take God's love, which correctly produces, protects and cultivates all things in Nature, and assimilate and utilize it in our own mind and body.

This revelation may have been only a momentary event, but it was the first such experience that he had ever had. It revolutionized the Founder's life and gave birth to Aikido.

From Aiki-Jujutsu to Aikido

Tracing the Founder's eighty-six years of study, we find that he was deeply interested in *budo* when he was young. He had gifted ability. Then came his pilgrimage throughout the world of jujutsu beginning in the middle of the Meiji era (1868–1912), during which he also devoted himself to the sword and other weapons, and the study of religions. Then, at last, the truth burst upon him.

The *budo* which he attained through his experience he later named Aikido.

When we look back to the old records and scrolls, in a few cases, we come across words like "a technique of aiki" or "aiki throw." But their explanations are abstract. "Don't be *aiki*-ed by the opponent." That is, don't drawn into the opponent's 'spirit harmony.' It is quite doubtful that a deeper meaning of the word was understood.

It was the Founder who clarified the superior way of Aikido as a separate entity in the society of *budo*—a society whose the members tended merely to emphasize techniques and strength. He asserted: "It is the way of *budo* to make the heart of the universe our own and perform our mission of loving and protecting all beings with a grand spirit. The techniques of *budo* are only a means to reach that end." The Founder, having thoroughly studied *budo* and acquired its essence through his severe training, first set up above all a goal for spiritual guidance and then fused the techniques of Aiki into the "stream of spirit, spirit power, or soul power." He gave life to the highly technical and spiritual side of Japanese *budo* within the society of man.

The Founder was the first who ever indicated clearly the world of Aiki and revealed its aim. From *jujutsu* to *do* (techniques to the Way)— this is the way to evolve endlessly toward the goal set up by the Master.

DEVELOPMENT OF AIKIDO

Busy Days at Ayabe

When the Founder was living at Ayabe, Wanishaburo Deguchi would announce to everyone he met, "There is a hell of a great warrior at my place." Probably because of this, various people visited his house. Vice Admiral Seikyo Asano was one of them. Admiral Asano arranged important contacts with the navy for the Founder and later served as his guide when the Founder moved to Tokyo.

Hidetaro Kubota, Yutaka Otsuki, Sogetsu Inagaki, Gunzo Oshikawa, Yoichiro Inoue, were all his students. Kubota (present name, Nishimura; a sixth-grade holder of judo) was a student of Waseda University at the time. He was a leading figure in the student judo field, and influenced many people to study Aikido, including Kenji Tomiki and Nobubumi Abe.

He recalls:

> When I was a student at Waseda Higher School, I heard of Prof. Ueshiba from Rev. Deguchi of the Omotokyo religion. Not expecting he could handle himself well, I attacked him. It was the carefree spirit of my youth that drove me to do it. I was amazed that he was so strong. After that time I occasionally served as a private secretary to the Founder.

The Founder's activities became very wide spread. After returning from Tokyo, he went to Osaka and Kyushu. He was constantly on the run with his many invitations. However there was no permanent training place (*dojo*) at that time.

The Master Meets Admiral Takeshita

There was a man named Wasaburo Asano who had an influential position on Deguchi's religious board. Admiral Asano was his brother. He met the Founder and wished to introduce the true value of his art to many others. He consulted with Admiral Isamu Takeshita, who was his classmate at the Naval Academy. The admiral, being fond of *budo*, requested the Founder to come to Tokyo. The two met at the mansion of businessman Kiyoshi Umeda. He had the same temperament as the Founder and became one of his earnest sponsors. After that time he often requested the Founder to come to Tokyo. Through the introduction of Admiral Takeshita, Count Gonnohyoe Yamamoto had an opportunity to see the Founder in action. He was astonished with his art of using the spear.

This event was followed by others which brought more noble people into his classes. A twenty-one day course of training was offered at the Aoyama Palace for those members of the Emperor's guard who were fifth-grade holders or above in judo or kendo. A temporary dojo was set up at the mansion of Ichizaemon Morimura. Groups of selected people from various fields began to visit the dojo.

Move to Tokyo: Training at a Rented House

The Founder's family moved from Ayabe to Tokyo during early 1927. They rented a two-storied house of five rooms at Sarumachi, Shiba Shirogane for 55 yen a month. Kiyoshi Yamamoto, a son of Count Gonnohyoe, and Admiral Takeshita helped them.

The billiards room of Prince Shimazu's mansion was remodeled and offered as a dojo. About that time, the daughters of Takeshita, Shimazu, Yamamoto and other nobles earnestly began to train.

In the first part of 1928 the Founder moved again. Among the students during that time, there were such admirals and generals as Takeshita, Eisuke Yamamoto, Sankichi Takahashi, Gengo Momotake, Ban Hasunuma, Nobutake Kondo and well-known people in financial and political circles. Iwao Kasahara, the student judo champion, entered the Founder's classes about then, too. Aiki captured public attention as a new *budo* just then appearing in the city of Tokyo.

The Founder was invited to be a *budo* teacher at the Naval Academy, and most of the teachers and students of the Academy studied under him. First class actors and dancers, including the late Kikugoro, came to learn the body movements of Aiki.

The applicants were many. Among them were Yoichiro Inoue, who had been raised by the Founder since he was small; Takeshi Nishimi, a sixth-grade holder of judo, who was the first *deshi* in Tokyo; Hisao Kamata, Kikuo Kaneko, and others.

The number of followers increased. It became impossible to receive any more of them. He moved again to Shiba Takanawa Kurumamachi in 1929, but this house also became too small within six months. At last the construction of a formal dojo and residence was discussed and an executive committee was quickly appointed.

A fairly large house situated on a hill in Mejiro was selected as a temporary residence to be used during the time the Headquarter's Dojo was being constructed.

A Visit by Professor Kano

It was a memorable event when Professor Jigoro Kano, founder of judo, visited this temporary house with his assistant, Professor Nagaoka and others. A good many high grader holders of judo had personally visited Master Ueshiba, but no one had been officially dispatched from the Kodokan, Kano's dojo and the headquarters of the judo movement. After seeing the Founder's Aikido in action, Mr. Kano is said to have remarked, "This is my ideal budo." He later revealed his feelings to his staff in this way.

> "To tell the truth, I would like to engage Ueshiba here at the Kodokan, but since he is a master in his own right, that will be impossible. Therefore I'd like to dispatch some able men from our art to study with Ueshiba."

It was not long after when Nagaoka came to study along with Minoru Mochizuki and Jiro Takeda. Nagaoka began to slack off after a brief period of study for various reasons, one of which was his age. Mochizuki, however, has continued to concentrate on the study of Aikido.

Completion of Kobukan Dojo

As the roll of new students gradually increased the training became so intense that the owner of the Mejiro property complained that even the beams of the house had begun to learn Aikido.

The new 80-mat dojo located at the present site in Ushigome (presently Shinjuku) Wakamatsu-cho was finally completed in April of 1931. It was named the Kobukan.

The Founder set up strict precautions to prevent the misuse of Aiki and would accept as new students only those whose character was vouched for. He was not interested in advertising Aiki; even so, the dojo grew rapidly.

"Hell Dojo of Ushigome" and the Uchideshi

There were thirty or forty live-in students, *uchideshi*, at that time. Most of them were high-grade holders of judo or kendo, many weighing more than 80 kilograms. These men, quite full of vitality, would exercise so much and train so hard that the place became known as the "Hell Dojo of Ushigome."

The young apprentices were concentrating on their studies in the microcosm of the dojo, separated from worldly affairs. They were ambitious. They had an intense desire to learn the secrets of Aiki under the guidance of the Founder and gain insight into a higher way of life.

The seniors were Inoue and Kamata. The new leading figures were Hajime Iwata of Waseda University, Minoru Mochizuki and Aritoshi Murashige. They had been despatched from Kodokan. They made an earnest effort, day and night, to make a good atmosphere in the new dojo. However late they sat up, even till two or three in the morning, they would jump up at five and begin cleaning the floor.

Among the *uchideshi* living with the busy Founder and taking care of him, Kaoru Funabashi and Tsutomu Yukawa distinguished themselves. Warm-natured Funabashi could take breakfalls freely while holding a spear in his hands. Yukawa felt an abiding power in himself after ten years of Aikido study and could easily clap together two bales of rice. They had extremely opposite characters. These two men, now having since died, were always publicly and privately assisting the Founder.

About the period from 1933 to 1935, Shigemi Yonekawa, Rinjiro Shirata, Zensaburo Akazawa, and Gozo Shioda joined the "Aiki Budo" group. There were also Kenji Tomiki and Tesshin Hoshi, who came from judo. Tomiki studied under the Founder from the time he had been famed as "the Tomiki of the Waseda University Judo Club." He entered the teaching profession in his home town for a while after his graduation. However his attachment to Aikido was irresistable; he resigned his position and joined the students of Aikido again. His manner of studying was very sincere, and continued until he was appointed to a new post as a professor of the Manchukuo National Foundation University. Tesshin Hoshi was a judo teacher at a high school in Kii Province. He was easily handled with one hand by Aiki man Tsutomu Yukawa, one of his former students at the high school. He fell in love with Aiki, and studied intensively for two years. The exceedingly self-confident Hoshi reflected on his two year's hard study and deplored the fact that he could never be a match for the Founder, no matter what he might do.

Rinjiro Shirata, full of talent, was considered a prodigy and admired as the pride of Kobukan. A few episodes from his life may show the temperament of the *deshi* of that time. He knocked on the gate of the Master in 1933 and studied for five years, until he departed for the front lines with the army. Those were the most gallant days of the Kobukan. In 1934, one year after entering, he was despatched to the Okayama Branch of the Budo Enhancement Association with fellow *deshi* Mr. Hashimoto. They were challenged to a match by two locals who were boastful of their abilities. Shirata declined solidly saying, "There is no competition in Aikido. A match means killing each other. Moreover it is the principle of 'Aiki Budo' not to fight." They wouldn't listen to him. So he stood up from necessity and threw one of them and pinned his hands. He then joked, "You see? Can you resist the world of non-resistance?"

There was another *uchideshi* who was more than six feet tall. He had experience in professional *sumo,* the traditional Japanese-style wrestling. He boasted about his abilities and talked in a grandiose style. He was quickly and easily pinned by Shirata. After that he never spoke about *budo* in front of Shirata.

There are many others to write about, including the vigorous Gozo Shiota. The burning will and effort of all founded a tradition of fortitude at the Kobukan.

Establishment of Dojo and Branches

There was a lively old man named Kyugoro Kuroyanagi living at Ushigome Kagurazaka. He was deeply impressed with the Founder and rebuilt one of his houses at Fujimidai, making it into a dojo. He rented it as a branch dojo. People could take adventage of its favorable location.

Seiji Noma, leading publisher and moralist, respected the Founder's way of living and training as a warrior. He rebuilt his house and offered to lend it to the Founder. His son Kiyoshi, the first to become a students, devoted himself to hard training. He had vigorous energy because he had recently won a kendo championship in a contest held for the Emperor. Meanwhile earnest applicants and potential association members appeared in the Osaka Area. Soon a branch dojo was set up there.

Other dojo were then set up in various places. The Founder was kept busy visiting them. Occasionally, he stayed for only 10 to 12 days a month in the Tokyo Headquarters.

Budo Enhancement Association

On October 13, 1932 the Budo Enhancement Association (*Budo-Sen'yokai*) was born. The Founder took office as president.

A 150-mat dojo was set up at Takeda, Tamba Province, to receive energetic young students. The Founder bought an old house at Takeda and made it into the headquarters of the association. It was traditionally said that a party of Loyalists of the Restoration Period, persued by Shogunate officials, had killed themselves by *harakiri* in the house. People used to call it the "Ghost House."

The efforts of the members finally yielded fruit, and branches of the association were set up in various areas of Japan. The Headquarters enrollment of students greatly increased, as well.

The Headquarters at Takeda were always crowded with 70 or 80 students and many episodes are related about them. Fujisawa handled an iron staff of 110 pounds with ease and skill. Ryosuke Suzuki carried a stone which weighed about 650 pounds to a river bed. Tsutomu Yuasa could bend back a six-inch nail. People of this caliber went back and forth, assembled and departed. They made the scene look like the center of the stock market.

Though many visited the Aiki dojo, they all knew the Founder engaged in extremely severe training. It was not a few times that the Founder immediately rejected demonstrating his art if he did not agree with the manners of the sponsors, or approve of those people gathered to watch. Those who entered the dojo in informal dress, or watched the training while standing, or folded their arms, were ordered out of the room.

Early Trainees

In accompaniment with the popularization of Aikido, the Founder grew concerned about any misuse of its techniques. He always required recommendations from two qualified persons in order to carefully select a student. Consequently many of the trainees were older or people of high position, and most of the young trainees were *budo* experts or children of prominent families. For that reason there were many private lessons given during non-scheduled hours. The *deshi* had to work almost without rest.

Prominent among the trainees were Marquis Toshitame Maeda and Dr. Kenzo Niki. Maeda was a real aristocrat. He had an attendant remove his shoes for him and help him put on his training uniform.

On the contrary Dr. Niki used to surprise the apprentices at five in the morning. He would propose an exercise and throw the *uchideshi*. As he executed each movement he would recite old Japanese sayings; "bending willows to the wind," "pouring water into a sieve;" things which indicate the movements of spirit power in Aiki. Then he would hurry home. The *deshi* who had been thrown would not be completely awake until the time the doctor left. Recalling those days they say he was like a phantom.

The World Wrestling Champion of that time was Mangan of America. He was more than six feet tall and one day had a match with the Founder. He attacked with the so-called flying kick. The Founder threw him instantly and effortlessly. After that he became a student of the

Founder and visited him almost every day for some time.

Later the locations at which instruction was given in Osaka included the Sumitomo Club, Asahi Newspaper and the Police Department. Mr. Yukawa taught during the Founder's absence.

Organizing a Foundation

Training in Aiki took president over all other kinds of *budo*. Kendo was practiced by the young Aikido members. They entered a contest, won, and brought the championship cup of the Imperial Moral Association back to the Founder. People in the *budo* field, including kendo and judo men, often visited the Aiki dojo. "Aiki Budo" was enhanced and more clearly understood by the general public. In 1939 reorganizing the Kobukan Dojo into the Kobukai Foundation was proposed. Incorporation was officially approved in 1940. Isamu Takeshita took office as the first president.

In the period of the Konoe Cabinet in 1940 the Budo Promotion Committee was organized. The Minister of Welfare was the chairman. The Founder was appointed a member of the committee. He was also despatched to Manchuria as a member of the Japanese *Budo* Delegation for the tenth anniversary of the founding of Manchukuo.

A professional *sumo* champion, Tenryu, became a *deshi* at Kobukai Dojo for about two and a half months. It was also about this time when "King Te" of Mongolia, during his visit to Japan, went all the way to Tokyo to satisfy his keen desire to see Ueshiba's Aiki arts.

In 1939 and 40, Koichi Tohei and Kisaburo Osawa, joined the Aiki dojo. But World War II soon broke out in 1941. As the situation grew more demanding the leading *uchideshi* were gradually called to military service. The once talent-filled Kobukai Dojo became quiet. It was about this time that the name "Aikido" came into official use.

Outdoor Dojo at Iwama

"If you own a *dojo* you will be pressed with various business matters such as management and other affairs, and become less devoted to *budo*. Then your skill will decrease." This was the Founder's cherished belief. For that reason he never lost his original spirit of a disciple. He was always faithful to the Way. His burning desire to know *budo* was always strong. Managing dojo was a secondary matter. As soon as the Headquarters in Tokyo was established, he sought new land free from the administrative problems of the city training place. "*Budo* and farming," a favorite theme of the Founder finally materialized in an outdoor dojo of Aiki at the town of Iwama, Ibaraki Prefecture, where the present Ibaraki Aikido Dojo is located.

The Founder insisted that an "Aiki Shrine" be erected first. Later a 40 mat dojo was built near by in the 72,500 square meter plot. This shrine became the sanctuary of Aikido. As the war intensified, the Founder went back to farming at this place, preached the Way, and taught earnest students who had heard of him and asked for instruction. This kind of life continued even after the end of the war. He matured further in mind and continued to refine his Aikido techniques.

Post-War Years

Though the talented Aikido men were scattered because of wartime service, the Instruction Department of Kobukai was still active under the direction of the author, who is the Master's successor, and Kisaburo Osawa. It offered courses in various places.

Following the war came the Occupation, and with the Occupation came a complete prohibition of *budo* activities. It was outlawed. Expecting rebirth some day, reorganization of the foundation was planned in order to respond to any new circumstances which might develop. A preparatory council was held on November 22 of 1945 at the Tokiwa mansion in Marunouchi, Tokyo. Fifty-three persons, including Prince Konoe (ex-premier), attended. At this council the official name of the organization was changed to "Aikikai" (the "Aikikai Foundation") and new officers were elected.

The new Foundation was approved on February 9, 1948 and the restoration of Aikido got off to a quiet, but solid beginning.

AIKIDO TODAY: A WORLD-WIDE PHENOMENA

Although Aikido was born in Japan late in the first quarter of this century, it made its first big jump into the world arena only in the early 1950s, after the liberalization of the post-war occupation regulations which banned all training in martial activities. Today, however, it is said that the number of trainees world-wide has reached one million; an exceptional growth that is definitely continuing.

PRE-WAR PERIOD

It was in 1922 that the Founder of Aikido, Ueshiba Morihei, began teaching the "Way" he would later name Aikido. From that year until 1945 and the end of the World War II, he dedicated his most strenuous efforts to enriching the content of his art and promoting it, mainly inside Japan.

However, during this turbulent period immediately after the birth of Aikido, the social and political background of the times had significant influence on the way the art progressed. Morihei mainly intended to spread Aikido to a very limited group of intellectuals and others of high social standing and never went quite so far as to suggest that it be spread to the general public. Therefore, all instruction was done by The Founder himself or under his strict supervision. He was thus too busy to exert any great or general influence on society.

POST-WAR PERIOD

After the end of the World War II, the changing times brought major reassessments of the administration policy of Aikido. In 1948, the government in the form of the Ministry of Education formally recognized a new body, the Aikikai Foundation (Zaidan Hojin Aikikai), as the sole official, national organization dedicated to the promotion of the art of Aikido. At that time Founder Ueshiba Morihei put his son, Kisshomaru, in charge of all matters including the administration of the organization and the spreading of the art. He himself had decided to remain in his country retreat outside Tokyo where he could exert himself singlemindedly toward making greater strides in the content of Aikido itself. It was there that he had built the Aiki Shrine (Aiki Jinja) as a spiritual focus of his movement. The Shrine honors the Shinto gods whom he viewed as the guardians of Aikido. (After his death in 1969 the Founder's own spirit was also enshrined there.)

Having been given responsibility for the art as a whole, the author, Ueshiba Kisshomaru, decided to popularize Aikido, not only in Japan, but among the general public all around the world. He took as his goals the fostering of a correct understanding of the art and its greater development. With these aims in mind he set about the tasks of establishing instruction methods, constructing an organizational framework, modernizing administration procedures, and so forth.

DOMESTIC GROWTH

By about 1955, the completion of a functioning administrative organization lead to social exposure that marked a strong step in spreading the art nation-wide. From the beginning of the nineteen sixties, university student Aikido organizations began to be formed until at present (in 1984) nearly 200 Japanese universities have Aikido clubs which receive instruction from teachers sent to them from the Aikikai Foundation.

In 1976, the "All Japan Aikido Association" was inaugurated to enhance mutual friendship and interaction among Japanese Aikido practitioners whether they belong to one of the existing Aikido associations, a club sponsored by some business organization, or the Self Defense Ministry Aikido Association. The Aikikai Foundation continues to play its central role as the umbrella organization in correctly spreading the art in Japan.

INTERNATIONAL GROWTH

In the meantime, the international development of Aikido has shown strong development in many nations on every continent. The main reason for the art's great and growing popularity seems to be its unique and substantial spiritual element. Many non-Japanese trainees feel that these deeper components of martial art are more prominent in Aikido than in the other Japanese budo that have spread abroad.

Beginning in the early 1950s, visits by various experts in the art stimulated the first signs of a "take off" of Aikido as an international phenomena. Initially, it was introduced into Hawaii, in the United States, and France, in Europe. Its deep, oriental spirituality immediately captured the minds of intellectuals and the art spread around the world in almost no time.

In 1975 a preparatory committee met in Midrid to discuss the formation of an "International Aikido Federation."

About thirty countries were represented. Then, in 1976, the Federation was formally inaugurated and began functioning. As of this writing in 1984, more than forty national Aikido federations and organizations have joined.

The art is especially flourishing in the United States; France, Italy, England, West Germany and other Europian countries; and Brazil in South America. Recent years have seen growth in Southeast Asia, Australia and other places. There are three major Japanese martial arts that have become most popular outside of Japan; Judo, Karate, and Aikido. Despite its relatively short history, Aikido is said to be attracting the most attention of late because of the high standard of its content. (See World Map, p. 166.)

THE HOMBU DOJO

As we have seen, there are numerous Aikido organizations inside Japan, including the "All Japan Aikido Association" and "All Japan Student's Aikido Association." Internationally, the previously mentioned "International Aikido Federation" and its regional administrative units are evolving on a great scale. Nevertheless, the recognized center of all these organizations remains the "Aikikai Foundation" in Japan and its training facilities known as the "World" Aikido Headquarters Dojo (Aikido Hombu Dojo).

The Founder Morihei opened the "old" Hombu Dojo at the present location (17-18 Wakamatsu-cho, Shinjuku-ku, Tokyo-to, Japan 162) in 1931. In 1968, the single-storied wooden structure was replaced by a large, 5-story dojo that is more suited to the needs of the greatly increased number of practitioners. At present, about 600 trainees attend the daily classes. In addition, there are about 400 officially recognized branch dojo around Japan, not including those affiliated with the previously mentioned subsidiary organizations. The total number of practice sites is thus in the area of 1,200 to 1,300.

The Aikikai Foundation issues grading certificates and serves as a central registration and distributing office for such gradings. Certificates of "black belt" ranks are issued over the name and seal of the present "Doshu." Doshu is the title of the hereditary leader of the Aikido world, the direct decendent of the Founder. The present Doshu is the author, Ueshiba Kisshomaru.

The Hombu Dojo also sends instructors abroad regularly and its interaction with overseas dojo has become closer and more frequent thanks to the support from the International Cultural Exchange Foundation, the Japan Maritime Promotion Association, and other generous groups. Today, the Aikido Headquarters Dojo, headed by Dojo-cho (Director) Mr. Osawa Kisaburo, carries out administrative activities on an ever broadening scale that occupies the vigorous activity of some thirty full-time *shihan* (licensed teachers) who have gathered there around the second Doshu.

(Please refer to the History section for further details about the history of Aikido and the Hombu Dojo.)

AIKIDO AROUND THE GLOBE

❶JAPAN
❷KOREA
❸TAIWAN
❹HONG KONG
❺MACAU
❻PHILIPPINES
❼THAILAND
❽BURMA
❾SINGAPORE
❿MALAYSIA
⓫INDONESIA
⓬PAPUA NEW GUINEA
⓭AUSTRALIA
⓮NEW ZEALAND
⓯MADAGASCAR
⓰SOUTH AFRICA
⓱LEBANON
⓲TURKEY
⓳EGYPT
⓴FINLAND
㉑SWEDEN
㉒NORWAY
㉓DENMARK
㉔POLAND
㉕GERMANY
㉖CZECHOSLOVAKIA

㉗HOLLAND
㉘BELGIUM
㉙LUXEMBOURG
㉚FRANCE
㉛SWITZERLAND
㉜AUSTRIA
㉝ITALY
㉞MONACO
㉟YUGOSLAVIA
㊱GREECE
㊲SPAIN
㊳PORTUGAL
㊴UNITED KINGDOM
㊵IRELAND
㊶MOROCCO
㊷ICELAND
㊸CANADA
㊹U.S.A.
㊺MEXICO
㊻BRAZIL
㊼URUGUAY
㊽ARGENTINA
㊾CHILE
㊿TAHITI (FRANCE)
51 HAWAII (U.S.A.)

AIKIDO AND OTHER *BUDO*

"What is the difference between Aikido and judo? And how about karate?" These questions are always asked during Aikido demonstrations. When you read the section on techniques you will learn the details.

Generally speaking, however, we can say that judo employs techniques of holding at the sleeves or collar, and takes advantage of a chance to throw the opponent. On the contrary, in Aikido the moment of contact is the decisive time for action. At first we stand apart, spacing ourselves and responding supply to the opponent's movements with Aikido techniques. Here there is no grappling or jostling with each other. It is possible to see a greater difference when compared with karate. The movements of karate, in general, can be resolved to thrusting and kicking. Hence most of the movements seem to be in straight lines, although some circular movements are included. Aikido has thrusting and kicking also, but its movements vary. The essence of Aikido techniques lies in complete circular and spherical motion. Straight movements in Aikido are rare.

Movements which are common to those of Aikido are more easily found in Japanese swordsmanship rather than in judo or karate. Although Aikido appears very different from swordwork, its movements are all based on those of the sword. It will be easier to explain the techniques of Aikido from the rationale of swordsmanship than from that of other arts. The Founder always stated:

> "Those who study Aikido, if holding a sword, must maneuver according to the techniques of Aikido swordwork, and if holding a stick, according to the techniques of Aiki stick action. A sword or a staff is an extension of the body. So unless you can handle it as if it were alive, you have not studied true Aikido."

The way of training in Aikido shares something in common with swordwork. In sword use, from the beginning of the fight to the end, there is always a distance of about two meters between the opponents. In Aikido, although you are not holding swords, you check the opponent at the moment the spacing becomes advantageous for you. Handling the sword in Aikido is based on the technique of advancing the whole body in an oblique form; this is somewhat different from the techniques of modern Japanese sport kendo.

As explained before, the Founder studied various kinds of *budo;* it is natural that they were adapted into the techniques of Aikido. But because the Founder acquired something beyond them, the essence of Aikido differs from that of other arts.

Occasionally the training of Aikido is misunderstood as simply being the training of forms *(kata).* But the variations of Aikido techniques are too numerous to be considered as such. If Aikido is practiced as mere form the essence of Aikido — "the movement of Nature is the movement of ourself" — can not be reached.

The Founder therefore said:

"There is no form and no style in Aikido. The movement of Aikido is the movement of Nature — whose secret is profound and infinite."

So it is essentially different from some of the other *budo* which cling only to forms. When we use the word "form," we mean that the techniques of Aikido are a series of endless spiritual forms. They are unified so closely with each other that they cannot be divided. This is beyond the concept of "form" in the conventional sense. The techniques of Aikido, as we can therefore see, are different from those of judo, kendo or karate, but its spirit is in accord with the secrets of these other arts.

DYNAMIC SURVEY OF AIKIDO

The techniques of Aikido are rationally structured from a dynamic viewpoint. They may be outlined as follows.

The human body, in motion, becomes like a spinning top. When not in motion the body is in the stable posture of an equilateral tetrahedron. This triangle-stance is the ideal posture from which to start the techniques of Aikido. When the movement begins the body becomes like a spinning top. In this sense the techniques of Aikido should reach a state in which you can change the opponent's CENTRUM by your own spherical motion which revolves around your CENTRUM. Thus you maneuver and spin off your opponent with your motion.

There is an old saying preserving a secret of jujutsu, "Push when pulled, and pull when pushed." It is clear from the following odes how the founders of the old jujutsu *ryu* taxed their ingenuity:

> Softness is the mind of a willow
>> Which turns the force of the wind against itself.

> If suppleness and strength were the essence of force,
>> Instruction would be much easier.

> Suppleness is the way to be strong;
>> Learn, thus, its exquisite utility.

These odes illustrate the principle of suppleness. Jujutsu literally means "the techniques of suppleness," while judo means "the Way of suppleness".

When the same concepts are explained by the principle of Aikido, it is, "TURN when pushed, and ENTER when pulled." (See section on techniques.) This circular motion is different from the straight movements of jujutsu. It has more variety. When it is fully utilized in *budo,* it leads to another more effective area. This is the development of spherical motions which consist of centrifugal and centripetal forces.

For this reason you and the opponent are not in dualistic opposition in Aikido but are one unit in which both are under your control. Both are completely controlled by the centrifugal force away from you and the centripetal force toward you. When such a spherical motion is continued as a systematic unity, the graceful rhythm and circular movement unique to Aikido appear. For example, the force which is used in the ENTERING THROW checks the opponent's right hand with your HANDBLADE from a RIGHT-OBLIQUE POSTURE, flowing off his *KI* as you enter on your left foot to his right side. You continue turning your body rightward on your left foot in a sweeping motion to unbalance his body, and then, changing your body leftward, you enter again on the right foot. When this kind of powerful, continuous and spherical motion is carried out by every part of the body, the force of individual parts is joined together and executed systematically in natural, circular, spherical, and spiral-like ways. The rotation must be flexible and accurate, with a stable rock-like balance serving as the center. It is like a windmill which responds to a slight wind — even one which normally could not be felt by a human body — and keeps rotating. Or it is like a top whose force of rotation extends to every part yet simultaneously concentrates and stabilizes its mass around the axis, supporting it — the top therefore maintains its balance.

By this action it spins off or draws in everything it touches. Similar examples in natural phenomena are powerful whirlwinds and whirlpools.

For these reasons it can be more easily understood why Aiki techniques of leading and throwing are based on movement from the hips. The opponent is involved in this action of centrifugal and centripetal forces which you execute and is therefore placed in an unstable situation. He finds himself turning around the outer circle of your top-like movement. This puts her into a "state of having an unstable body position." For example, in the CORNER DROP, as soon as you have your left wrist grasped by the opponent's right hand, you stretch out your left hand powerfully to his right rear corner and stop his right foot with your right hand. This prevents the movement of the opponent's CENTRUM. When his right hand is pulled to his right rear while his CENTRUM is stopped, his form becomes unstable and he falls. The opponent, in actuality, is moving around the outer circle of your CENTRUM, and hence is unstable. When we analyze this motion and observe body positions and relationships of force, we know that the forces of the techniques are delicately worked out and related. Another example is seen in the WRIST IN-TURN or NIKYO. You hold the opponent's wrist while you are constantly turning around your center. Consequently he moves around your outer circle with his body unbalanced. His wrist is bent toward the "direction of natural bending," thus he moves in the same direction. Most of the joint techniques of Aikido employ the moving of joints in the direction in which they bend naturally. It is different from ordinary reversal techniques, which hurt the joints by turning them in a direction counter to natural bending. These "natural bending" techniques are used because the principles of circular and spherical motion are rationally utilized in Aikido. When we observed the Founder in action and considered these force relationships, we saw that the movement of his hands and feet traced spherical shapes as his motion accelerated around his stable hips. When holding a stick, his body and the stick took on the appearance of a spherical body. The stick looked almost as if it were alive. Thus when we train ourselves in Aikido we must study technique in order to be like a pyramid (equilateral tetrahedron) when not in motion, and to become like a spherical body when moving. The spherical body must be versatile, keeping its power contained, harmonizing the centrifugal and centripetal forces, just as a rubber ball rolls down a slope, lively bouncing no matter how bumpy the slope may be. These kinds of force relationships are worth studying further from the standpoint of Aiki Dynamics, but in training ourselves we should learn the state of "no-mind," and not be shackled with the analysis of theories.

AIKIDO AND HEALTH

Most *budo* originated from a kind of physical training program, developed into self-defense arts, and then were refined into *budo*.

A physical fitness program may be compared to preventive medicine programs. If we move our body adequately and if the movement agrees with Universal Nature, we will have a well-conditioned body and will not be affected by disease. Among the excellent warriors of whom we have heard, longevity is an outstanding characteristic. That they have practiced physical fitness during their training in *budo* certainly is related to this longevity.

When we consider various physical fitness programs we will soon discover the value of Aikido. The movements of Aikido agree with the laws of Universal Nature which include a flowing flexibility and the keeping of a stable CENTRUM. The aim of Aikidoists is to be one with the Universe, in complete self-control. When we have self-control, we also have a posture which is completely alert. By exercising our whole body we approach improved health.

Dr. Katsuzo Nishi, a man famous for his health-improvement theories says:

> "When we watch people involved in Aikido, we see that their stance is like an equilateral tetrahedron. We watch them begin the characteristic spherical rotation. They change in various ways,

extending and drawing, without losing their centered balance. Theirs are completely controlled figures. When the body is controlled, it is most healthy."

This is the type of body we see when skilled Aikidoists are in action. The continuous and flexible motion based at the hips is like the performing of a dance. It is a graceful spherical motion. Observing such finger, wrist, foot and hip movements, all coordinated with the breath, we see that they agree with physical improvement ideals. The movements of every part of the body are unified into a systematically controlled whole.

First, BREATH POWER, which is the basic resiliant power of Aikido, is extended from the CENTRUM. This naturally relaxes one's strength, which has stiffened various parts of the body. It becomes the basis of constructing a flexible but stable posture for both young and old.

Secondly, some cases have shown that spherical motion based on the hips, when it is executed with a stable posture, is helpful for correcting bone structures, especially the spinal column. For example, those who had drooping shoulders and bent spinal columns as a result of previous illnesses found their condition completely corrected after a year of adequate Aikido exercise.

Thirdly, the delicate movements of Aikido help accelerate blood circulation at every joint of the body and give adequate stimulation to some inner muscles which are not generally used. For example, when KNEE WALKING, the toes are neccessarily moved and bent. Since most people in our modern age wear shoes, the exercise of such understimulated muscles will be beneficial for good health.

The basic PINNING TECHNIQUES; the First, Second and Third Teachings; all give impulse to the inner muscles. Skilled Aikido trainees' deep and subsurface muscles are well developed, and as elastic as a rubber ball. The Founder said that the joint exercises in the PINNING TECHNIQUES are to remove the "dust" which has accumulated around the joints.

In Aikido, techniques related to individual parts of the body are necessarily related to the whole. There are no radical techniques which use strength suddenly, or immediately cease using power. The spirit fills the whole body from head to toe in every case. Here lies the secret of

Aikido in preserving a healthy body.

To exercise the body in this way, with adequate moderation, will no doubt lead to better health. It should be understood, however, that Aikido is *budo* and not a physical fitness program. Aikido improves health only as a result of its practice as *budo*.

RULES DURING PRACTICE

At the Headquarter's Dojo in Tokyo the following RULES DURING PRACTICE are posted for all to see and learn:

1) One blow in Aikido is capable of killing an opponent. In practice, obey your instructor, and do not make the practice period a time for needless testing of strength.

2) Aikido is an art in which one person learns to face many opponents simultaneously. It therefore requires that you polish and perfect your execution of each movement so that you can take on not only the one directly before you but also those approaching from every direction.

3) Practice at all times with a feeling of pleasurable exhilaration.

4) The teachings of your instructor constitute only a small fraction of what you will learn. Your mastery of each movement will depend almost entirely on individual, earnest practice.

5) Daily practice begins with light movements of the body, gradually increasing in intesity and strength; but there must be no over-exertion. That is why even an elderly person can continue to practice with pleasure and without bodily harm; and why he will attain the goal of his training.

6) The purpose of Aikido is to train both body and mind and to make a person sincere. All Aikido arts are secret in nature and are not to be revealed publicly, nor taught to hoodlums who will use them for evil purposes.

First it is proper to obey the instructor and remember his instructions; rise above yourself. No matter how much you may study, if you cling to yourself you will not develop your ability.

Secondly, *budo* is for countering any attack from any direction at any time. When you are merely ready for only one opponent, without being prepared for others, it will be only a common fight. A tight, on-guard posture with an immovable spirit is the basis of every exercise in *budo*. People generally say, "That man behaves irreproachably," or "An excellent artist is completely on guard." Those who study Aikido should thus spend their daily life thoroughly on guard, even if they are not consciously watching every direction around them.

Thirdly, it is fairly painful to keep on studying earnestly. But if you keep up the discipline of *budo* without tiring, you will at last reach a really enjoyable stage. Some people misunderstand that it is best to suffer while studying, but real study is pleasant at all times. Concentrating ourselves, not having any harmful experiences, we are able to enjoy our practice sessions.

The forth rule relates to the assimilation of techniques. Aikido has a few thousand variations in its techniques. Some students are apt to chase after an accumulation of quantity rather than quality. However when they look back on themselves, they are sorry to learn that they have gained nothing. Soon they lose interest. As innumerable variations of each technique are possible we instructors always emphasize the significance of "repetition" to beginners. When you practice each basic technique, over and over again, you master it and then are able to use the variations.

When the Founder first came to Tokyo, among his earnest students was Admiral Isamu Takeshita. He wrote down all the techniques that he learned under the Founder. They amounted to more than two thousand, and yet there were more. He was deadlocked, finding that he could do none of them well. After careful consideration over several days, he understood the meaning of the Founder's advice "You should study, using the sitting exercises as your base." He practiced it and then at last became able to manage the techniques so well that he could acquire others which he had not yet been taught by his instructor. For an elderly man of sixty years, it is the same: repetition of the basics is the secret of improvement, no matter how awkward or unskillful one may be.

The fifth rule is not to contradict nature. Excessiveness is to be avoided in anything. Moderation is the key. No matter how little the excess is, the whole posture and the condition of the body will be unbalanced.

Young, lively students are apt to have the idea that they will not be strong unless they force their power. This is not true. Natural practice creates true strength. For this reason, it was possible for Dr. Niki, a man more than eighty years old, to practice Aikido.

Lastly, the aim of Aikido is not to merely produce a strong body but to create an integrated person. Any educated person knows how brute strength is meaningless in our present-day advanced civilization. For this reason the Founder forbade Aikido to be misused and severely cautioned everyone. He would not permit the publication of his art's techniques and required introductions and guarantees for each student.

In summary, those who wish to study Aikido should have a righteous and fair mind, obey their instructors, and study naturally. As a matter of consequence, their techniques will be skillfully cultivated in such an atmosphere and a noble character will be created.

WORDS OF THE FOUNDER

As *ai* (harmony) is common with *ai* (love), I decided to name my unique *budo* "Aikido," although the word "aiki" is an old one. The word as it was used by the warriors in the past is fundamentally different from mine.

Aiki is not a technique to fight with or defeat the enemy. It is the way to reconcile the world and make human beings one family.

The secret of Aikido is to harmonize ourselves with the movement of the universe and bring ourselves into accord with the universe itself. He who has gained the secret of Aikido has the universe in himself and can say, "I am the universe."

I am never defeated, however fast the enemy may attack. It is not because my technique is faster than that of the enemy. It is not a question of speed. The fight is finished before it is begun.

When an enemy tries to fight with me, the universe itself, he has to break the harmony of the universe. Hence at the moment he has the mind to fight with me, he is already defeated. There exists no measure of time — fast or slow.

Aikido is non-resistance. As it is non-resistant, it is always victorious.

Those who have a warped mind, a mind of discord, have been defeated from the beginning.

Then, how can you straighten your warped mind, purify your heart, and be harmonized with the activities of all things in Nature? You should first make God's heart yours. It is a Great Love, Omnipresent in all quarters and in all times of the universe. "There is no discord in love. There is no enemy of love." A mind of discord, thinking of the existance of an enemy, is no longer consistent with the will of God.

Those who do not agree with this cannot be in harmony with the universe. Their *budo* is that of destruction. It is not constructive *budo*.

Therefore to compete in techniques, winning and losing, is not true *budo*. True *budo* knows no defeat. "Never defeated" means "never fighting."

Winning means winning over the mind of discord in yourself. This is to accomplish your bestowed mission.

This is not mere theory. You practice it. Then you will accept the great power of oneness with Nature.

Don't look at the opponent's eyes, or your mind will be drawn into his eyes. Don't look at his sword, or you will be slain with his sword. Don't look at him, or your spirit will be distracted. True *budo* is the cultivation of attraction with which to draw the whole opponent to you. All I have to do is to keep standing this way.
Even standing with my back toward the opponent is enough. When he attacks, hitting, he will injure himself with his own intention to hit. I am one with the universe and I am nothing else. When I stand, he will be drawn to me. There is no time and space before Ueshiba of Aikido — only the universe as it is.
There is no enemy for Ueshiba of Aikido. You are mistaken if you think that *budo* means to have opponents and enemies and to be strong and fell them. There are neither opponents nor enemies for true *budo*. True *budo* is to be one with the universe; that is, to be united with the Center of the universe.

A mind to serve for the peace of all human beings in the world is needed in Aikido, and not the mind of one who wishes to be strong or who practices only to fell an opponent.

When anybody asks if my Aiki *budo* principles are taken from religion, I say, "No." My true *budo* principles enlighten religions and lead *them* to completion.

I am calm however and whenever I am attacked. I have no attachment to life or death. I leave everything as it is to God. Be apart from attachment to life and death and have a mind which leaves everything to Him, not only when you are being attacked but also in your daily lives.

True *budo* is a work of love. It is a work of giving life to all beings, and not killing or struggling with each other. Love is the guardian deity of everything. Nothing can exist without it. Aikido is the realization of love.

I do not make a companion of men. Whom, then, do I make a companion of? God. This world is not going well because people make companions of each other, saying and doing foolish things. Good and evil beings are all one united family in the world. Aikido leaves out any attachment; Aikido does not call relative affairs good or evil. Aikido keeps all beings in constant growth and development and serves for the completion of the universe.

In Aikido we control the opponent's mind before we face him. That is we draw him into ourselves. We go forward in life with this attraction of our spirit, and attempt to command a whole view of the world.

We ceaselessly pray that fights should not occur. For this reason we strictly prohibit matches in Aikido. Aikido's spirit is that of loving attack and that of peaceful reconciliation. In this aim we bind and unite the opponents with the will power of love. By love we are able to purify others.

Understand Aikido first as *budo* and then as a way of service to construct the World Family. Aikido is not for a single country or anyone in particular. Its only purpose is to perform the work of God.

True *budo* is the loving protection of all beings with a spirit of reconciliation. Reconciliation means to allow the completion of everyone's mission.

The "Way" means to be one with the Will of God and practice it. If we are even slightly apart from it, it is no longer the Way.

We can say that Aikido is a way to sweep away devils with the sincerity of our BREATH instead of a sword. That is to say, to turn the devil-minded world into the World of Spirit. This is the mission of Aikido. The devil-mind will go down in defeat and the Spirit rise up in victory. Then Aikido will bear fruit in this world.

Without *budo* a nation goes to ruin, because *budo* is the life of loving protection and the source of the activities of science.

Those who seek to study Aikido should open their minds, listen to the sincerity of God through Aiki, and practice it. You should understand the great ablution of Aiki, practice it and improve without hinderance. Willingly begin the cultivation of your spirit.

I want considerate people to listen to the voice of Aikido. It is not for correcting others; it is for correcting your own mind. This is Aikido. This is the mission of Aikido and this should be your mission.

INDEX